MW00527799

'Dick Woolcott was Australia's leading diplomat for a generation and had a remarkable range of contacts around the world. He also possesses a great sense of humour from which even prime ministers were not spared.'

GOUGH WHITLAM

'If I was making a film on a global crisis and wanted an actor for the central role of a cool, classic, intelligent and witty diplomat, I would cast Dick Woolcott. He has an infectious sense of humour.'

PHILLIP ADAMS

'As a cartoonist I have regarded Dick Woolcott, not only as one of Australia's most successful diplomats but one who also has that precious gift of humour and the ability not to take himself or his profession too seriously.'

BILL LEAK

'Dick Woolcott has been a most outstanding diplomat. Relaxed and jovial, he is also blessed with a quick sense of humour which, I am delighted to see, he is now sharing with readers.'

ANDREW PEACOCK

For my family, friends, and colleagues past and present
in the world's foreign services who are blessed
with a sense of humour.

UNDIPLOMATIC ACTIVITIES

Richard Woolcott

Illustrations by David Rowe

SCRIBE
Melbourne

Scribe Publications Pty Ltd
PO Box 523
Carlton North, Victoria, Australia 3054
Email: info@scribepub.com.au

First published by Scribe 2007

National Library of Australia
Cataloguing-in-Publication data

Woolcott, Richard, 1927- .
Undiplomatic activities.

ISBN 9781921215384.

1. Woolcott, Richard, 1927- . 2. International relations. 3. Diplomats - Australia.
4. Australia - Foreign relations - 1945-. I. Rowe, David. II. Title.

327.10994

Sections of the 'Liberian Dispatch' have been previously published in the *Bulletin* (1974), and in *The Hot Seat: reflections on diplomacy from Stalin to the Bali bombings* (Harper Collins, 2003)

www.scribepublications.com.au

Contents

Introduction

Laughter breeds good humour and is the best antidote to self-righteousness and rancour.
— Daniel Varé

I have devoted most of my working life to diplomacy. It is an important and serious business. Its failure often results in a resort to force that can have catastrophic consequences — as the situation in Iraq demonstrates. That noted, diplomacy should not be regarded as a sacred cow. Like any other profession, it has its quota of buffoons, snobs, and jesters, its pomposities, strange protocols, and its bizarre moments that are worthy of satire. As Peter Ustinov once remarked, laughter would be bereaved if snobbery died.

The idea for this book came when re-reading Lawrence

Durrell's satire *Esprit de Corps: sketches from diplomatic life*, illustrated by V.H. Drummond, and first published in London in 1957.

The bookstores and libraries these days seem well stocked with works on international affairs, including my own, *The Hot Seat: reflections on diplomacy from Stalin's death to the Bali bombings*, published in 2003. This book is different. Its primary aim is to amuse rather than explore the complexities of foreign relations. In 1938, Daniel Varé wrote in his book, *Laughing Diplomat*, 'like marriage, mothers in law and seasickness, diplomats are the butt of music hall wit. This is all to the good. Laughter breeds good humour and is the best antidote to self-righteousness and rancour'. I find this still to be the case.

Australian politics has become dour and humourless. Consequently, our diplomacy tends to have followed suit and is more prim and proper than it used to be. The late Anna Russell, the comedienne and musician and who died in 2006, once described herself in jest as an expert in 'musical depreciation'. I have always appreciated the role effective diplomacy can play and so I hope this book will not now cast me as an expert in diplomatic 'depreciation'.

A sense of humour and of the ridiculous is an essential item in the survival kit of today's diplomat. Indeed, to be able to laugh at the world and at ourself is a blessing. I remember seeing the original *Beyond the Fringe* review in

London. My wife and I were both suffering from an unpleasant reaction to inoculations prior to travelling to Moscow, but laughter banished our depression and lifted our spirits. We laughed until it hurt at the delicious satire of Dudley Moore, Peter Cooke, Alan Bennett, and Jonathan Miller.

Once, when flying first class on Qantas to Bangkok in those days of relative self-importance, I found myself sitting next to a prosperous-looking man. He was sipping a whisky and reading the *Bulletin* magazine. I was drafting a speech for our foreign minister to deliver in Thailand. Every few minutes my travelling companion burst into guffaws of laughter. Observing that I was attempting to work, he apologised, adding, 'Have you read this? It's a hilarious report about the inauguration of the president of Liberia written by our diplomatic representative at this event.' I realised immediately he was reading my infamous dispatch, 'All Hail Liberia, Hail', which the foreign minister at the time, Paul Hasluck, had banned having found no place for levity in the serious business of diplomacy. Suppressed, it was naturally leaked to the media. I did not confess that I was the author, but I have always envied comedians and felt a modest glow of satisfaction that something I had written was giving enjoyment and amusement to another person. This book seeks to draw on such moments, including the Liberian dispatch.

It is said that a good cartoon is worth a thousand words. Over the years, diplomacy has ranked second only to politics as a source for our cartoonists and I am delighted to join with David Rowe, one of Australia's best, in the hope of bringing some laughter into the lives of readers.

DUBIOUS DIPLOMATIC BEGINNINGS

This book might never have happened. My diplomatic career could have been aborted before it really started and while I was still what was called 'a diplomatic cadet in training'.

Although we were all graduates of other universities, trainees were expected to complete another two-year course at the Canberra University College. Most of us were housed at Gungahlin, now a large Canberra suburb but then an old two-story rural homestead on the road to Yass that had been converted into a university hall of residence. Despite the fact that we were under the supervision of a very conservative warden and obliged to pass exams at the end of the course before we could be appointed to the public service, these were wild, rebellious days.

Together with another trainee I became the founding co-editor of the student association's newspaper which we named *Woroni*. It still exists today. *Woroni* is an aboriginal word meaning mouthpiece, and we used it to make fun of the university and the government. A recent book, *The Making of the Australian National University*, noted that *Woroni* became known for intelligent and provocative comment. One article in particular attracted considerable interest and was quoted in Sydney and Melbourne newspapers. It referred irreverently to the recently constructed American war memorial in front of the Department of Defence — a very tall column topped by an eagle — under the headline 'Phallus in Blunderland'.

In those days, I also fancied myself as a potential cartoonist and as a composer of limericks. This harmless pun on *Alice in Wonderland* and two signed cartoons in which I was rash enough to send up both the prime minister and the leader of the Opposition, then Robert Menzies and Ben Chifley, resulted in my being given a 'serious warning' by the senior officer in the department responsible for the management of the diplomatic trainees.

But it was another infamous incident that most threatened my incipient diplomatic career and which has since entered Canberra mythology — the felling of the flagpole at Gungahlin. It was described in *The Making of the Australian National University*:

> Professor Jim Davidson, who was then a resident, was celebrating with three cadets the appointment of one of them, Richard Woolcott, to a diplomatic posting in

> Moscow. After an evening on the town, they rolled up in front of the homestead about midnight in Davidson's Riley tourer, continued their revels in the common room with much din and bawdy songs, and brought proceedings to a climax about one in the morning by chopping down the flagpole at the front of the building with the evident intention of using it as a battering ram.

Our foolish behaviour was motivated by a number of things: in part by our frustration at having to complete the diplomatic studies course when we were already graduates; in part by the isolation of living in a country homestead posing as a residential university college; and in part by the artificiality of the role of gentleman students that we were expected to play, involving sherry before dinner and wearing academic gowns and ties at dinner. Moreover, the warden's dedication to the British monarchy and to flag-raising ceremonies irritated those of us involved in axing the pole. Even in those days we were dedicated republicans. The story has, however, become apocryphal; the claim that the flagpole was carried up the stairs and used as a battering ram to break down the door of the terrified warden is an embellishment.

Several of the others were expelled from Gungahlin for their participation in the incident. Bill Morrison (who went

Beggars can't be choosers.

on to become defence minister in the Whitlam government) and I were more fortunate, and avoided their fate because our postings had already been settled. Shortly afterwards, we left for London to undertake a Russian interpreters' course at the London University School of Slavonic Studies before moving on to Moscow.

My third diplomatic misadventure was on the voyage to London. We were at sea for a month on full pay, small as it was then, and without having to take any leave. We stopped at a number of exotic ports such as Colombo, Aden, Suez, and Marseilles and it was a memorable holiday — for several reasons. At Marseilles, after exploring this fascinating Mediterranean city, we missed the ship and had to hitchhike across France to London, sharing a truck for much of the journey with a consignment of pigs — beggars can't be choosers. In the end, we arrived at Tilbury in time to meet our ship, claim our luggage, and report to Australia House. We were miraculously on time and the senior foreign affairs representative was none the wiser.

In retrospect, I suppose I was fortunate that the management of the Department of External Affairs in the early 1950s was more tolerant of such wayward and undiplomatic activities than I expect would be the case in today's more tightly managed service. There may well have been no such book.

CHAPTER 1

Diplomacy past and present

How should you govern any Kingdom that know not how to use Ambassadors. — William Shakespeare

Historically, diplomacy is probably the world's second oldest profession. Indeed, some would argue it has much in common with the oldest profession. Harold Nicholson, the British diplomat, author, and politician suggested that diplomacy began at the dawn of history when the inhabitants of some caves realised that it might be mutually advantageous to come to an understanding with neighbouring cave-dwellers about the limits of their respective hunting territories.

Homer wrote of the dispatch of a diplomatic mission to Troy. Herodotus described an Egyptian king who sent a secret message to an ally by diplomatic courier long before the birth of Christ. As he would need to pass through potentially hostile territory, the king had his courier's head shaved and the message tattooed on the bare scalp. He was dispatched only when his hair grew back. This method had the advantage not only of hiding the message from unintended readers, but also from the courier. I suppose the modern equivalent is multiple sealed enveloping with the last marked, 'To be opened by addressee only'.

The practice of employing resident ambassadors appears to have started when the capital of the Roman Empire was moved to Constantinople in 359 CE. It was here that what is often referred to as 'Byzantine' diplomacy took root. Unfortunately, it came to be associated with often corrupt and venal methods.

Modern European diplomacy probably dates back to Cardinal Richelieu, the French cleric and statesman who formed the first distinct foreign ministry in Paris in 1626. Richelieu's confidant, Friar Pere Joseph, conducted the most difficult negotiations during the Thirty Years' War and, because he always wore a grey habit, he became known as the *éminence grise* — the power behind the throne. Through him a new phrase entered the language of diplomacy and, indeed, the vernacular.

Also in the seventeenth century, Shakespeare recognised the potential value of diplomats. He wrote in *Henry VI*, Part

3, 'How should you govern any Kingdom that know not how to use Ambassadors?'

In the most famous handbook on diplomacy, *A Guide to Diplomatic Practice*, Sir Ernest Satow wrote in 1917, 'Diplomacy is the application of intelligence and tact through the conduct of official relations between the governments of independent states.' We will hear more about the importance of tact later.

Even now, early in the twenty-first century, diplomacy and the activities of embassies, high commissions and consulates seem to be shrouded in mystery to many of our citizens. Once, when addressing a group of secondary school students about a career in diplomacy, a boy told me that he wanted to be a diplomat because he would like to sign a treaty and meet attractive female foreign agents.

Sir Henry Wotton, one of Queen Elizabeth I's ambassadors, penned the infamous comment that 'an ambassador is an honest man sent to lie abroad for the good of his country'. In the Australian context, it has been suggested that some of our diplomats, like our convict forbears, have been transported to faraway places for this country's good.

I fear that the mythology surrounding diplomacy has never really recovered from its Byzantine associations and such oft-quoted jibes as Wotton's. Even today, the idea lingers that to refer to a person as 'diplomatic' is mildly

The power behind the throne.

pejorative, suggesting somebody who is smooth but devious, even if not as deceitful as the politicians it is the official's lot to serve. When a lady in England said she would like her daughter to marry a diplomat and a gentleman, a good friend with some experience of diplomacy said, 'Well my dear, she will have to commit bigamy.'

A French colleague once said to me that ambassadors have now less space and authority, and that increasingly 'we have become a combination of travel agent, messenger boy, and inn keeper'. He added that one of his former presidents, Georges Pompidou, had once outraged his diplomats when he said that one of their most important attributes should be the ability to balance a cup of tea and a slice of cake at the same time.

When overseas, an ambassador is expected to run a sort of guesthouse for visiting ministers and to arrange tedious functions for them. Whereas in the past our diplomats would be preoccupied with reporting on the political, personal, and occasional amorous intrigues in the government to which he or she was accredited, now they are forced to attend to a host of more mundane activities such as consular cases, tariff negotiations, disarmament, fisheries, and smuggling. These days they also have something in common with commercial travellers and advertising agents in that they must spend a large proportion of their time promoting Australian products and tourist attractions.

On the other hand, some ambassadorial duties have been discontinued, such as the power under the Marriage Act to solemnise marriages of Australian citizens overseas. I officiated at three marriages, the shortest — between an exotic dancer at a West African nightclub and the cook at an Accra hotel — lasted two weeks. I was a more successful celebrant in the Philippines as the two Australians I married at the official residence in 1980 are still together.

Peter Ustinov, whom I once had the pleasure of entertaining, described a diplomat as little more than 'a headwaiter who is allowed to sit down occasionally'. Lester Pearson, a former Canadian prime minister, said more generously that, 'a good diplomat can say no in such a way that it sounds like yes'.

The popular media still tends to portray diplomats as anachronistic figures able to ignore parking regulations. They are often seen as meddling in other peoples' affairs often dressed in formal attire and bedecked with decorations, and — champagne glass in hand — hosting parties for their own amusement at the taxpayer's expense. The Egyptian ambassador to the UN, with whom I had become friendly, once gave me a tie with a camel motif, and asked rhetorically, 'What is the difference between a camel and a diplomat?' The answer, 'A camel can work for two weeks without drinking. Some diplomats can drink for two weeks without working.'

While such images may contain a grain of truth about European diplomatic life in the nineteenth century, Australian diplomacy is even today sometimes unfairly afflicted by them. But diplomacy is mainly about trying to secure what we want from our foreign relationships and, to that extent, it is not unlike our aims in business, family relationships, and life itself. The diplomat and historian Sir Charles Webster made the more illuminating comment that diplomacy 'consists in obtaining the maximum national interest with a minimum of friction and resentment'.

The Roman emperor Caligula appointed his horse a consul. While modern diplomacy has not suffered indignities of this order, many unsuitable persons have been appointed to senior diplomatic posts around the world.

In the United States you can still purchase ambassadorships by making generous financial contributions to the political party in power. The most recent case, which attracted the anger of the *New York Times* and state department professionals, was President Bush's appointment of Sam Fox to Belgium in 2007.

The appointment of Maxwell Gluck to Sri Lanka in 1957 was a notorious case which became a symbol of the misuse of ambassadorial appointments as payoffs for campaign contributions. At his Senate confirmation hearing he was, under forensic questioning from Senator Fulbright, hazy about where Sri Lanka (then called Ceylon) actually was, and he did not know the name of the prime minister or any minister in the government to which he was to be accredited.

In Australia it is still not possible to buy an ambassadorship, but we have had numerous political appointments over the years. Some have been good, some indifferent, and some — such as that of Senator Vincent Gair to Ireland in 1974 — appalling. John Howard has in fact made about a dozen non-career political appointments, the most recent being former senator Amanda Vanstone who was posted to Rome as part of a deal to drop her from Cabinet early in 2007. It was widely criticised in the media and satirised in a bogus film poster advertising the winner of the '2007 Cynic's Award' — 'A Roman Holiday production starring Alessandro Downer and Amanda Vanstone in Giovanni Howard's *La Dolce Vanstone*'. I must confess a family interest in that she replaced my son Peter, a career officer.

Woody Allen once quipped that 'ninety percent of diplomatic life seems to be just showing up'. Depending on the task at hand, diplomacy can be very demanding or quite relaxing. There is a word in Japanese, *koroshi*, which means dying as a result of overwork. I do not know of any diplomat who has succumbed to it; from other better-known excesses, yes, but not from overwork. There have been occasions when I have worked around the clock with colleagues, for example when negotiating the communiqué on our first prime ministerial visit to China. At such times, I entirely sympathised with US secretary of state Henry Kissinger who was quoted in the *New York Times* saying, 'There cannot be a crisis next week, my schedule is already full.'

One of the more arcane aspects of diplomacy is nomenclature. If a government does not approve of another countries form of administration — even in some cases when it has been elected — it will often refer to it as a regime, for example the Iranian 'regime'. Countries also occasionally change their names for various reasons, such as sensitivity about their colonial past: Upper Volta changed to Burkino Faso; Ivory Coast became Cote d'Ivoire; Rhodesia became Zimbabwe. President Idi Amin was dissuaded from changing the name of Uganda to Id because a country of that name appears in a well-known comic strip, and it was also pointed out to him — rather bravely — that the people of Cyprus were called Cypriots and the people of Id might well be called Idiots.

There have been many discussions about the correct word to describe foreign service officers. While traditionalists like Satow prefer diplomatist, diplomat is in general use now. Lady Marjorie Tange, the wife of Sir Arthur Tange, a formidable secretary of external affairs, wrote in her guide to etiquette, *Notes for Wives of Officers of the Department of Foreign Affairs,* that the husband of a foreign service wife should always be called a diplomatist and that, 'strictly speaking anyone could be called diplomatic (that is tactful) without being a diplomat'. She suggested that the word diplomat originated with sub-editors seeking a shorter word to fit into a headline.

In diplomacy, titles have always been important. An Australian ambassador is still referred to as His Excellency. This does not normally extend to spouses. Indeed, the wife of one of our ambassadors in South-East Asia exposed herself and her husband to some ridicule when she persuaded him to send a circular to the staff insisting she be addressed as Her Excellency. *Diplomatitis* is the name commonly used in describing an affliction in which status goes to one's head.

The church, in my view, does somewhat better than diplomacy in the matter of titles: the Pope is called Your Holiness; the Orthodox Patriarch is addressed as Your Beatitude; even a bishop is called Your Grace. But of all ecclesiastical titles I would prefer to be called Your Eminence, the title bestowed on cardinals by the Catholic Church. At the other end of the scale, I was once given a card in Africa on which the official was wonderfully described as Chief Assistant to the Assistant Chief.

Unlike in Australia, an American ambassador keeps the title for life. When an American friend accepted an ambassadorial appointment in the last weeks of the first

Bush administration, I asked him why he had done so as it seemed likely that Clinton would win the election and he would have to resign only weeks after taking up the post. 'Ah', he said, 'but I will keep the title and be called *the honourable* for the rest of my life.'

While works such as Lady Tange's handbook on etiquette were undoubtedly well intentioned, they were wide open to the barbs of cynics. Indeed, although it was marked 'Not for Distribution Outside the Government Service', the *Canberra Times* contrived to obtain a copy in July 1972, and published extracts under the engaging headline *Lady T's Titbits ... or how to shut off the grog without guests really noticing* (in my experience an almost impossible task at a function attended by Australians). The first three words of the headline were attributed to a group of younger and less submissive wives who, even in the 1970s, were reluctant to be regarded as unpaid appendages to their husbands' diplomatic careers.

'Two for the price of one' was — and still is, although in fewer cases — a fair description of what is expected of diplomatic wives. But in the twenty-first century, the two-income family has become normal and there are a growing number of women in the foreign service who hold senior positions, including heads-of-mission appointments. There are still, however, many wives of diplomats — including my own — who sacrificed good independent careers to provide full-time support for their husbands, at home and abroad. I even have a visiting card of a well-qualified lady, which simply has the words under her name, 'wife of the Ambassador of …'.

In diplomacy, as in life, success has many fathers, while failure is an orphan. Two ministers and several prominent public servants, for example, claim authorship of the highly successful Colombo Plan under which thousands of Asian students were educated in Australia. The ranks of those who supported the war in Iraq are thinning rapidly, except for those political leaders in the United States, Britain, and Australia who find it difficult to admit a political folly. In the past, when a diplomat failed in a mission he was likely to be punished, occasionally even by death. How times have changed. Now after a failure one is quite likely to be rewarded with a decoration or moved sideways for standing down or for shouldering some of the government's accountability.

No diplomat, in my experience, has been penalised for failing to see an opportunity or for lack of initiative, and this undoubtedly leads to excessive bureaucratic caution. On the other hand, the failure to predict danger or identify risk can have dire career repercussions, so there is a temptation to exaggerate the severity of the consequences of a proposed course of action. Both trends encourage paralysis, or lack of balance, rather than imagination.

Throughout my own career I tried to strike a balance between excessive caution and innovative prediction. Gareth Evans hosted a farewell dinner for me at Parliament House in 1992 when I retired as head of the Department of Foreign Affairs and Trade. As is customary on such occasions, libellous revelations mixed with excessive praise flowed as freely as the drinks. Referring to the old nostrum about the ape who 'the higher he climbs, the more he bares his arse', Gareth added kindly, if not entirely accurately, that during my career I had kept my 'backside admirably well covered'.

In fact, one of his predecessors had me removed from the Canberra scene and posted to far away West Africa because, at a briefing for the Melbourne *Age*'s editorial staff, I had the temerity to suggest that in my 'personal opinion' the government was overdue in extending diplomatic recognition to the People's Republic of China. I was told that if public servants had personal opinions they should keep them to themselves. The government recognised China five years later. Also, penning the Liberian dispatch could hardly be described as covering my backside.

To many people, part of the mystery of diplomacy is the location or nature of many countries, even quite large ones. Indonesia is a case in point. Although by population it is the largest Islamic nation on earth, there is a surprising ignorance about it. On an overseas flight I once asked an

American businessman whether he had been to Indonesia. 'No,' he replied, 'but I have been to Bali.' Some years ago, I was in a Boston taxi driving through heavy rain between the airport and Tufts University with a friend from the Asia Society in New York. To illustrate his view that American's lacked knowledge of Asia, he applied what he called his taxi driver test. 'Do you know where Indonesia is?' he asked. The driver frowned and replied, 'Sorry, buddy, I don't go outside the main suburbs when it's raining hard.'

I was surprised to discover that President George Bush had never been outside of the United States before he was elected president. It is probably apocryphal, but a senior member of the US State Department told me that when President Bush was planning his brief visit to Africa in 2005, a White House aide had asked why the president was including Botswana in such a brief African itinerary. The president is said to have replied, 'I'm told there are a lot of Bushmen there.'

As well as adaptability, a sense of humour, a good tailor, a strong liver, and a supportive family I believe that a diplomat needs to have as many strings to his bow as he or she can muster. Whether it is literature, music, art, film, or sports and games, they can all be used to help break the ice. One never knows when some shared interest or ability might provide access to or consolidate vital diplomatic contacts.

I have used them all without shame and with varying degrees of ability to cement relationships, including playing chess with former president Garcia of the Philippines, and even golf with Lee Kuan Yew and Greg Norman. One has, however, to be selective. Talking to a senior Russian official about cricket is unlikely to be useful. On the other hand, discussing squash or wrestling with former US defence secretary Donald Rumsfeld could certainly cement the relationship and therefore improve access to him — although it would not be productive to discuss American strategy in Iraq in a headlock on the mat in the Pentagon gymnasium.

Whatever a diplomat's role may have been in the old days, it has certainly changed. As the number of sovereign states has increased, the pressure on foreign services to deal with them has grown. There are now 193 members of the United Nations compared with 154 in 1984 when I was in New York and we last secured election to the Security Council. This expansion, along with the growth of international trade and the rapidity of modern communications, means that today's diplomat is very much busier.

During an extended diplomatic tour to no less than fifteen countries, prime minister Gough Whitlam had been criticised in the Australian media for what was said to be excessive international travel. I recall that Gough was browsing through the London *Times* while we were in the anteroom waiting to meet with the Dutch prime minister. Noticing a report that Grenada, Guinea-Bissau, and Bangladesh had just been admitted to the United Nations Gough snorted, 'Have you seen this, comrade? Three new countries are joining the UN. They are creating these damned countries faster then I can visit them.'

Diplomacy has also become more dangerous than it used to be. Traditional diplomatic notes of protest tend to have been replaced, or at least reinforced, by chanting, stone throwing mobs outside an embassy. Although terrorism long predates 11 September 2001, terrorists increasingly regard embassies and diplomats as visible targets of opportunity.

Despite the amusing anecdotes and incidents, and the formalities and the pomposities that occasionally mask the valuable activities of diplomats that I recount in this book, we should not forget that diplomats have a demanding role to play. They are vital not only in the service of the national interest, but also in confronting and containing the many issues which beset the international community.

CHAPTER 2

Protocol, alcohol, and geratol

Those who matter don't care. Those who care don't matter. — George Bernard Shaw on status and protocol.

The former foreign secretary of the Philippines, General Carlos Romulo, once described diplomacy as based on 'protocol, alcohol, and geratol'. Apart from protocol I assume this was an oblique reference to diplomats' easy access to duty-free alcohol when serving overseas and to a medical preparation intended to reduce the risk of the transmission of certain diseases.

Protocol, in its various guises, remains at the core of diplomacy. It can simply refer to an official document, such as a protocol to an agreed treaty. But it is the other meaning relating to official formality, status, order of precedence, etiquette, and such weighty matters as where one is placed at the dinner table — what the French call *placement* — that gives rise to satire. I have witnessed an ambassador arrive for a dinner hosted by a colleague only to turn and walk out after studying the table plan because he was not seated according to his precedence. George Bernard Shaw is reputed to have commented on protocol, 'Those who matter don't care. Those who care don't matter.' It is not quite that simple.

An example of the archaic language of protocol — which also puts beyond question the fact that the English monarch and not the governor general is our head of state — is related to the credentials of an Australian ambassador to another country. My credentials appointing me as ambassador to Indonesia read:

> Elizabeth the Second, by The Grace of God Queen of Australia and Her other Realms and Territories … nominate some Person of approved Wisdom, Loyalty, Diligence and Circumspection (*that's meant to be me!*) to represent Us … Now Know Ye … We do by these Presents nominate, constitute and appoint him the said Richard Arthur Woolcott Esquire to be Our Ambassador Extraordinary and Plenipotentiary at Jakarta …

AUSTRALIA

John R Kerr

Elizabeth the Second

by the Grace of God Queen of Australia and Her other Realms and Territories, Head of the Commonwealth:

To all and singular to whom these Presents shall come, Greetings!

Whereas *it appears to Us expedient to nominate some Person of approved Wisdom, Loyalty, Diligence and Circumspection to represent Us in the character of Our* Ambassador Extraordinary and Plenipotentiary *at* Jakarta

with the especial object of representing the interests of Australia.

Now Know Ye *that We, reposing especial trust and confidence in the discretion and faithfulness of Our Trusty and Well-beloved* RICHARD ARTHUR WOOLCOTT, ESQUIRE, *have nominated, constituted and appointed, as We do by these Presents nominate, constitute and appoint him the said* RICHARD ARTHUR WOOLCOTT, ESQUIRE, *to be Our* Ambassador Extraordinary and Plenipotentiary *at* Jakarta *for the purpose aforesaid. Giving and Granting to him in that character all Power and Authority to do and perform all proper acts, matters and things which may be desirable or necessary for the promotion of relations of friendship, good understanding and harmonious intercourse between Australia and the* Republic of Indonesia

for the protection and furtherance of the interests confided to his care; by the diligent and discreet accomplishment of which acts, matters and things aforementioned he shall gain Our approval and show himself worthy of Our high confidence.

And We therefore request all those whom it may concern to receive and acknowledge Our said Trusty and Well-beloved RICHARD ARTHUR WOOLCOTT, ESQUIRE, *as such* Ambassador Extraordinary and Plenipotentiary *as aforesaid and freely to communicate with him upon all matters which may appertain to the objects of the High Mission whereto he is hereby appointed.*

Witness Our Honourable Sir John Robert Kerr, Companion of the Order of Australia, Knight Commander of the Most Distinguished Order of Saint Michael and Saint George, Knight of the Most Venerable Order of the Hospital of Saint John of Jerusalem, one of Her Majesty's Counsel learned in the law, Our Governor-General of Australia,

this Twenty Fifth *day of* February *in the year of Our Lord One thousand nine hundred and* Seventy Six *, and in the* Twenty Fourth *year of Our Reign.*

By His Excellency's Command,

[signature]

The same old-fashioned regal language was used when I was appointed to the Philippines. My credentials were signed by Sir John Kerr for the Indonesian appointment, and by Sir Zelman Cowen for the Philippines, and both were described as the queen's 'witness' to the appointment, and as 'Our' (meaning Elizabeth II's) Governor General of Australia.

Senior diplomats representing their countries overseas — and not only those with large egos — welcome the surety provided by protocol because the order of precedence and the relative status it imposes reduces the scope for disagreements. The importance of precedence was summed up in an early *Punch* cartoon in which an angry diplomat in black tie says to a colleague, 'You cad, you farted in front of my wife.' The colleague replies, 'I am sorry. I did not know it was her turn.'

While on this indelicate subject, Queen Elizabeth II often accompanies visiting heads of state in the open royal carriage along the Mall to Buckingham Palace if the weather is not inclement. On one occasion, when a visiting president was riding with the queen, one of the rear horses drawing the carriage lifted its tail and broke wind loudly. Discomforted by this lapse of equine dignity, Her Majesty said, 'Oh, Mr. President. I am sorry.' Her visitor, somewhat confused, hesitated and replied, 'Think nothing of it Your Majesty. For a moment, I thought it was the horse.' This story may well be apocryphal, but it was told to me by a member of the Royal household.

Despite all the care that is taken to ensure that correct protocol is observed and honoured guests are not offended, it can all break down with a failure of language. My wife and I received an elegantly printed gilt-edged invitation to a reception to be held at the historic Osu Castle in Accra by the chairman of the Presidential Commission to mark the fourth anniversary of the revolution which overthrew President Nkrumah. Somehow the words *desired* or *required* had been replaced and the invitation noted, 'An answer is not deserved.'

Diplomatic notes are a normal form of exchange between diplomatic missions and the governments to which

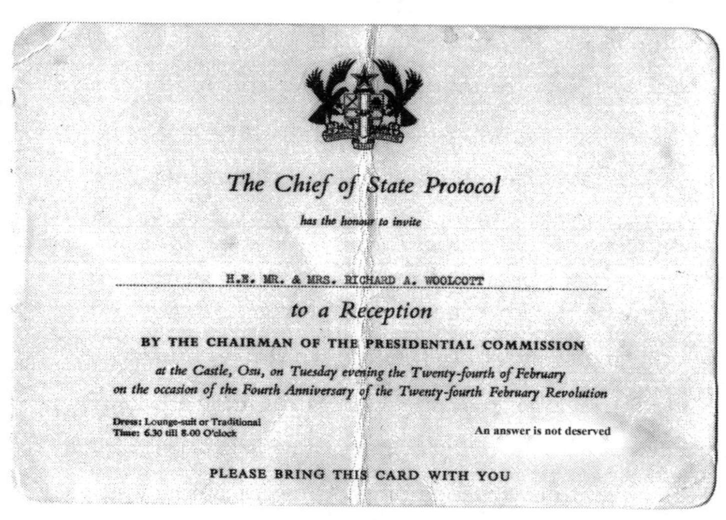

The Chief of State Protocol

has the honour to invite

H.E. MR. & MRS. RICHARD A. WOOLCOTT

to a Reception

BY THE CHAIRMAN OF THE PRESIDENTIAL COMMISSION

at the Castle, Osu, on Tuesday evening the Twenty-fourth of February
on the occasion of the Fourth Anniversary of the Twenty-fourth February Revolution

Dress: Lounge-suit or Traditional
Time: 6.30 till 8.00 O'clock

An answer is not deserved

PLEASE BRING THIS CARD WITH YOU

they are accredited. They are usually couched in polite language, even when conveying dissent or unwelcome tidings. They usually begin with the words, 'The Embassy of … presents its compliments to … and has the honour to inform …'. A significant exception, and one of the most colourful and popular episodes of Russian history, venerated by every Russian schoolboy and commemorated in a well-known painting by the Ukrainian painter Elias Repin, is the reply of the Zaporozhye Cossacks to a demand for surrender from the invading Turkish Sultan Mahmud IV:

> O sultan, turkish devil and damned devil's kith and kin, secretary to Lucifer himself. What the devil kind of knight are you, that can't slay a hedgehog with his naked arse? The devil shits, and your army eats. You will not, you son of a bitch, make subjects of Christian sons; we've no fear of your army, by land and by sea we will battle with thee, fuck your mother.
>
> You Babylonian scullion, Macedonian wheelwright, brewer of Jerusalem, goat-fucker of Alexandria, swineherd of Greater and Lesser Egypt, Armenian pig, Podolian thief, catamite of Tartary, hangman of Kamyanets, and fool of all the world and underworld, an idiot before God, grandson of the Serpent, and the crick in our dick. Pig's snout, mare's arse, slaughter-house cur, unchristened brow, screw your own mother!

> So the Zaporozhians declare you lowlife. You won't even be herding Christian pigs. Now we'll conclude, for we don't know the date and don't own a calendar; the moon's in the sky, the year with the Lord, the day's the same over here as it is over there; for this kiss our arse!
>
> Koshovyi Otaman Ivan Sirko, with
> the whole Zaporozhian band

Some three hundred years after Sirko had penned this note, another Russian, foreign minister Andrei Vyshinski, commended its style and frankness to his Western colleagues during a United Nations debate.

CHAPTER 3

Antics on the world stage

Why, then the world's mine oyster, which I with sword will open. — William Shakespeare

When governments, including our own, claim the support of the 'international community' for their foreign policy, they are often attempting to cloak their attitudes and those of their allies in unjustified respectability. If there is a measure of international community opinion it has to be the United Nations, because it is the only global institution in which all sovereign states, great and small, are present. Despite its shortcomings and clear need for reform, the UN remains the best hope for a more stable, peaceful, and less damaged world. But in order for it to be effective, it must have the commitment of all countries and their leaders.

I represented Australia for six years at the UN, including two years on its principal organ, the Security Council. Actually, I am starting to feel like I imagine a threatened species might feel — a dinosaur of Australian diplomacy. I was the last Australian ambassador to carry out this role and, sadly, we have been unable to secure election to the Council for over 20 years. During my time as our ambassador at the UN, I witnessed many amusing moments. In a debate on the need for a legal regime to govern activities in space, our solicitor general inadvertently referred to 'the useful pieces of outer space', instead of the 'peaceful uses of outer space'.

A particularly amusing episode involved our famous humorist Barry Humphries. A Sydney newspaper correctly reported that Humphries was involved in a movie modestly titled *Sir Les Saves the World,* in which his creation, Sir Les Patterson, played Australia's ambassador to the United Nations. In the final scene, Sir Les is addressing a packed General Assembly in New York. As his oration draws to a close, the president of the General Assembly, sitting behind Sir Les, strikes a match to light a cigarette just as the flatulent ambassador passes wind. The Assembly is engulfed in flame.

Although this seemed like a bit of inconsequential — if coarse — fun, the UN office in Sydney through its

The world will end with a bang, not with a whimper.

Canadian representative, George Ignatieff, protested to the Department of Foreign Affairs. The department requested that, as I knew Barry Humphries, I might seek to have the 'offending scene' removed from the movie. We were on the Security Council dealing with a range of serious issues at the time, including the Iran–Iraq war, but this was too good an opportunity to miss for comic relief. I sent a cable in reply to Canberra's request, headed 'The Winds of Change':

> Ignatieff seems to be over-reacting to *Sir Les Saves the World*. We certainly do not think that the minister should become involved. Nor does Woolcott consider he should try to use his suggested 'personal influence' with Barry Humphries to persuade him to delete the 'offending scene'. Moreover, he does not believe this would work.
>
> We think it would be a fruitless exercise to become officially involved in what will be a fairly coarse send-up of the United Nations which few people, inside or outside Australia, would be likely to take seriously. We also recall that in 1974 when Bruce Beresford was making *Bazza Pulls It Off* in London there was great concern in Australia House about a scene in which Australians in London celebrated Australia Day at the High Commission. As we recall that situation, the scene was not deleted from the film despite the strictures of the then Deputy High Commissioner, and

we are sure it was not taken seriously at the time and has since been forgotten.

The question of the logo could be resolved simply by having an artistic presentation of it, that is something that looked like the UN logo but which was in fact slightly different in detail.

While we attach importance to the dignity and the work of the United Nations, and while the scene described in the *Daily Mirror* may be regarded as somewhat uncouth, the United Nations is not beyond satire. We do not think we should risk turning a little satirical wind into a diplomatic gale. Also, actions of the type described in the 'offending scene' are not unknown in the General Assembly (although not, of course, on the fart of Australian representatives) but they usually pass with less explosive and dramatic results than Sir Leslie reportedly generates in the film.

Also, such scenes in entertainments are not without precedent. In the 19th century, a well-known French entertainer known as Le Petomaine broke wind professionally, even before the crowned heads of Europe, and a book has been written about his exploits. Indeed, it contains an account of him playing the 'Marseillaise' through a tuba in this manner.

As a final thought on this exchange, maybe T.S. Eliot was wrong. At least in this film, the world will end with a bang and not with a whimper.

The matter was quietly dropped and the film was released. The offending scene did not appear to attract particular interest.

Diplomatic life is not always serious and orderly. The Australian delegation to the session of the General Assembly in 1962, for example, included a number of younger men and women who were to do well in the foreign service, becoming heads of diplomatic missions in later years. Yet they were capable of unexpected and uninhibited behaviour. The Australian delegation's official reception, hosted by ambassador James Plimsoll, was held at the St Carlos Hotel on 52nd Street where our delegation was staying that year. After Plimsoll left the formal part of the function, the real fun began — and continued until the arrival of the New York police. A cricket match was played with wastepaper baskets as wickets, empty bottles as bats, and large ice cubes as balls. An Australian senator from Queensland — also a member of the delegation, and who had a well-known liking for alcohol — was involved in fisticuffs with a future Australian ambassador to Washington who believed the senator had propositioned his wife. But the most dramatic event was yet to come.

A young, attractive female third secretary from our mission attracted the attention of a number of guests, including the Somali deputy chief of mission. Somehow she became locked in a room with him at the end of the suite of rooms in which the function was being held. Her cries asking for help to open the door were heard by two noble Finnish diplomats. Finding the door unyielding, and emboldened by vodka, they decided to rescue the trapped maiden. Climbing out of a window they tried to move onto the ledge of the adjacent window behind which she was apparently trapped. But the first lost his balance and his grip, and fell. Fortunately, the awning of the Black Angus Steak House two floors below below broke his fall, much to the surprise of the guests, who, looking up from their steaks, were suddenly presented with a pair of legs protruding through the hole.

The second Finn was less fortunate. When he fell, he went through the already torn awning and landed on the footpath. The amazed diners did not know from what floor these bodies had fallen. Was it a suicide attempt? The police were called. Upstairs the party continued, with most guests unaware of the Finns' unsuccessful rescue attempt and fall. Meanwhile, the door had been opened and our third secretary had rejoined the party.

I shall always remember the moment when two large New York policemen appeared at the entrance to the reception. 'What's going on here?' one of them asked. 'Jim' McIntyre, our ambassador to Japan and Plimsoll's deputy on the delegation, was aware that the situation called for tact and diplomacy and said, 'This is the latter stage of an Australian official reception. Is there anything wrong?' 'Well, two persons have just crashed through the Black Angus Steak House awning two floors below where this party is being held. One has injured his leg and diners have reported the incident.'

I recall the slight figure of Jim between the two burly cops as he led them into the corridor to continue his explanation and to defuse the situation. From the back, however, it looked as though he was being led away by the police. A worried stenographer said to me, 'Why are those cops arresting the ambassador? He is actually quite sober.'

Fortunately the chivalrous Finns were not seriously injured and no charges were laid. But the matter did not end with a caution from the NYPD. The St Carlos Hotel management banned the Australian, Finnish, and Irish delegations — always a potentially volatile mix of nationalities — from staying there for some years. The next day, the Black Angus Steak House presented the Australian mission with a substantial account for damages and repairs.

An attempt to conceal the incident from Plimsoll by secreting the cost of damages in the expenses of the Australian official reception failed due to the vigilance of his secretary. If you have a difficult problem, refer it to a committee! And so, in the best traditions of the UN, the Black Angus Awning Committee (BAAC) was established

Falling Finns at the Black Angus.

to recompense the restaurant by collecting donations from Australians at the party. The secretary of the committee acted with humour and vigour. In one of the many notes pleading for contributions he said he was 'overawed' by the restaurant's demands, and that the Black Angus would certainly be 'overawned' if its demand were to be met in full.

To this day I do not know how the matter was resolved. After the assembly, I paid a modest contribution after returning to my post in Kuala Lumpur. When passing the Black Angus on subsequent visits to New York, I noticed that it looked prosperous under a splendid new green awning — the heroic falling Finnish diplomats only a nostalgic memory.

This delegation party will not be forgotten. Indeed the function attracted its own mythology in the United Nations and midtown Manhattan. After all, it is not every night that senior and normally serious diplomats plunge through the awning of a well-known restaurant. Most recently the event has been described, not entirely accurately, in the memoirs of Gerald Hensley, a former New Zealand diplomat and secretary of its Department of Defence.

The late Bob Katter, former Country Party member for Kennedy in Queensland, was a parliamentary member of the Australian delegation to the United Nations in the 1980s. Wearing his broad-brimmed Akubra hat and leather riding-boots, Katter certainly looked the part of a representative of outback Queensland, and he caused something of a stir at the UN. One afternoon, after a well-lubricated lunch, he was dozing off in the General Assembly when Dr Mohamad Mahathir, at the time prime minister of Malaysia, was criticising Western countries for the lack of respect often shown to early anti-colonial leaders. 'For example', he said, 'many in the West, including the media, represented Mahatma Gandhi as some sort of half-naked fakir.' Hearing the phrase, Bob suddenly snapped out of his doze, 'Jeez, Dick, can you get away with language like that in the General Assembly?'

Regrettably, Australia has moved away from its long-established commitment to the United Nations. In June 2002, Alexander Downer told the National Press Club that 'multilateralism is a synonym for an ineffective and unfocused policy involving internationalism at the lowest common denominator'. Previously he had dismissed the UN as 'irrelevant' when the Security Council declined to authorise the invasion of Iraq. Less than three months after the invasion Downer was calling on the UN to help clean up the mess the situation in Iraq had descended into.

In 1996, after failing in its last bid for election to the Security Council — defeated by both Portugal and Sweden — the humiliated government sought explanations from our New York and various other diplomatic posts. The wittiest answer — a simple one-liner — came from one of our ambassadors in Europe who replied in an email, 'The Butler did it.' Perhaps our lobbying tactics, including those of Richard Butler, our ambassador to the UN at the time, had something to do with our failure. But I suspect that Richard would deny it.

With the present discussion on Australian values, it is perhaps appropriate to recall that when I was last in New York, in June 2007, the record for the largest number of martinis consumed in a single day at the bar of the UN delegates' lounge — established by the deputy head of the Australian mission, John Hood, in 1961 — still stood. I suspect it will never be broken.

CHAPTER 4

Your obedient servant

Do not go out of your way to be witty.
— Sir Ernest Satow's advice to diplomats on writing dispatches.

In diplomacy, heads of missions give speeches to various organisations and report to their ministers on major events in their areas of responsibility. Some diplomats occasionally risk breaking the shackles of conformity with a little levity. Dispatches used to commence with the archaic salutation, 'Sir, I have the honour to report ...' and end with the quaint, 'I have the honour to be, Sir, your obedient Servant.' This traditional British practice led occasionally to frivolous misuse, and the Department of Foreign Affairs and Trade abandoned the practice in the 1970s.

Early in the Apollo space program, our ambassador to Indonesia — perhaps a disobedient servant — could not resist beginning a dispatch to the minister, 'Sir, I have the honour to report that, having been summoned to the Palace by President Sukarno, his first question to me was whether I knew if sexual intercourse was possible in a state of weightlessness.'

I penned a number of learned dispatches from various posts, most of which are no doubt gathering dust in the archives. However, as I mentioned in the introduction, the so-called 'Liberian dispatch' has enjoyed wide public readership. While serving at the Australian High Commission in Accra, I was asked to represent foreign minister Paul Hasluck at the fifth inauguration of President Tubman of Liberia in 1968. My report, 'All Hail Liberia, Hail', named after the the first line of the Liberian national anthem, was guaranteed notoriety inside and outside the department after Hasluck banned it. It was even published in the *Bulletin* in 1973. This is an edited version.

Sir, I have the honour to suggest that a sense of humour and a sense of the ridiculous are essential elements in the survival kit of the mid-twentieth century diplomat who is likely to find himself in one of the several ramshackle republics or comic opera countries which have been established on the ruins of the colonial system, or for other reasons made their appearance on the international stage.

In the serious business of diplomacy, there are, I trust, occasions on which a head of mission at an Australian outpost will, like the poets, be afforded a little license and a little levity in his reporting. Such an occasion should be the fifth consecutive reinauguration of President William Vacanarat Shadrach Tubman, leader of the True Whig Party, and President of the Republic of Liberia, at which it was my lot to represent Australia at the beginning of this year.

This West African happening was attended by representatives of 71 countries, as well as of the United Nations, the Organisation of African Unity, and the Vatican. One president, two vice-presidents, the crown prince of Ethiopia, the secretary-general of the OAU, six foreign ministers, and sixteen other representatives of ministerial rank also made the journey to Liberia.

John Gunther wrote that 'Liberia is sui generis', while Sir John Harris described it as 'a devil's paradise'. Perhaps it is both. It is also a sort of American stepchild and calls to mind images of tom-toms and top hats, of voodoo, of poverty, of lingering slavery (as late as the 1930s slaves were sold to Fernando Po and French Gabon), and the exploitation of black natives by black settlers.

The capital, Monrovia, despite its attractive situation on the Atlantic, can hardly be described as a beautiful city. An American travel agency is said to have arranged a sales promotion quiz recently. The first prize was a one-week paid holiday in Monrovia. The second prize was two weeks' holiday there. There are two seasons, the hot and the very hot. There is also a dry season during which it rains but not as continuously as it does during the rest of the year. It is humid, incredibly dirty and dilapidated with the exception of a few prestige buildings. Most of the town appears to be crumbling away with rot and rust. Traces of unmaintained American colonial architecture give parts of the city an atmosphere slightly reminiscent of William Faulkner's long summers of heat and decay in the southern states of the USA.

The main street boasts a number of lurid signs depicting bleeding rats and large cockroaches which advertise pest destruction. The city is indeed alive with pests of one sort or another. On returning to the hotel in white tie and tails from one of the ceremonies we witnessed a huge rat, which my wife at first took to be a basset hound, being clubbed to death on the doormat by enthusiastic bellboys.

While some of the better features of United States life are noticeable, such as the prevalence of airconditioning and showers, many less desirable aspects of American influence are also evident. Flamboyant cars (big fins and twin aerials are still in) in extraordinary colour combinations, such as cream and blue or chocolate and silver, speed through the narrow and uneven streets conveying important officials with their cigars and their mistresses to their places of work and pleasure.

The city is alive with thieves and during the inauguration

great precautions were taken at the Ducor Hotel to see that the foreign representatives left the country with more or less what they came with. To this end armed police clambered around the roof most of the day and night and, occasionally, they would appear during the night with acrobatic daring on a balcony from the roof above or the balcony below. One frightened Asian representative, who mistook a policeman for a robber as he swung over the balcony in the dim light, handed him his wallet containing $200 and neither the policeman nor the wallet were seen again.

The poverty in and around Monrovia is acute and obvious. Most of the population live in steamy, fetid congestion in rusted corrugated iron and clay hovels through which run a maze of red-rutted mud paths.

President Tubman is a shortish, plump, cigar-smoking, vain, omnipresent character. He is solid and stiff-necked and resembles an ebony puppet or a golliwog in horn-rimmed glasses. He carries a black stick and wears morning dress to the office. To an even greater extent than de Gaulle was said to be the embodiment of modern France or Prince Sihanouk the embodiment of Cambodia, President Tubman is Liberia. Nothing can be done or is done without his approval …

President Tubman is in the mould of the European benevolent despots, provided he is not crossed, who not unlike the Sultan of Brunei runs a small and backward state largely for his own amusement. The president rules by

Presenting credentials.

patronage and nepotism. He arranged the marriage of his eldest son to the vice-president's daughter to help check any political ambitions the vice-president might have nurtured. One story current while I was there was that the president had asked the vice-president in a lift at the executive mansion whether he had broken wind. The vice-president, who could be described as something of a hole in the political air, is said to have replied, 'No Shad, but I will if you want me to'.

The 'cult of personality', well known in retrospect in Stalin's Russia, Sukarno's Indonesia, and Nkrumah's Ghana is very evident in Liberia and still very much in fashion. Practically every second organisation and institution is named after President Tubman. At his inauguration everything from T-shirts to toilet paper was available in the Tubman motif. There were Tubman stamps, Tubman pins, Tubman badges, Tubman pennants, Tubman balloons, and Tubman dress material. Special fireworks made in Hong Kong even exploded President Tubman's image into the sky above the guests at the garden party. In his official biography, which he personally approved, it is stated that, 'If the Liberian people idolise him, it is because he has convinced them beyond the shadow of a doubt that his every effort, his entire life is devoted to their peace, prosperity, and happiness.'

In fairness, I should add that President Tubman has presence and charm. He smiles frequently and enjoys life.

He is hardworking and travels widely throughout his domain. Probably more than any other previous president — which is not saying very much — he has the good of his people at heart and appears to be respected, despite his ostentatious living.

Perhaps I was lucky to find myself flying to Monrovia since the original invitation to the Australian government to be represented had been dispatched by sea mail and had taken three months to reach Canberra. But arrive I did to commence one of the most extraordinary interludes the varied life of an 'ambassador extraordinary' could be expected to offer.

Each delegation to the inauguration was to be met at the airport by a liaison officer. If only the word were the deed in West Africa. In approximately a third of the cases, including my own, the liaison officer was not there. The Liberian ambassador to Ghana, who had been put in charge of reception arrangements at the airport (the wretched creature stayed there for five days and nights and never actually entered Monrovia), was most adroit in arranging for bewildered airways clerks to become 'temporary' liaison officers. Because our own liaison officer had not appeared there was no official car with an Australian flag and we set off at great speed in an ancient Renault commandeered for the purpose on the 50-mile trip from the airport to the city. It soon transpired that our 'stand-in' liaison officer knew nothing about the ceremonies to come while our driver seemed possessed by a fatalistic determination to join the burnt-out cars strewn along both sides of the road all the way into the city. Nevertheless, arrive we did at the Ducor Intercontinental Hotel, where the more fortunate of the foreign representatives were to stay …

The first event of the inauguration was a 'national thanksgiving and intercessory prayer service' at the First Methodist Church. This was an extraordinarily congested, confused, and theatrical affair. The church could only be approached through narrow streets and it seemed that approximately twice the number the church could hold had been invited. Like Melbourne trams after the football there was always room for one or two more inside. The temperature in the church climbed steadily until the conditions were like those in a Turkish bath, the difference being that most visitors were dressed in morning dress or dark suits. Florid-faced ambassadors dripped with perspiration in their overcrowded pews as the service dragged on for nearly two hours. Some relief was caused when the fifth pew groaned and then collapsed under the ample frames of the wives of the Liberian cabinet.

Bishop S. Trewen Magbe Snr, a Billy Graham in matt finish, preached a fiery but interminable sermon — or eulogy of President Tubman to be precise — in which he referred to the president as a man who combined in one body the talents of Lincoln, Gandhi, Kennedy, and Chief Luthuli. Anthems, responsive readings, doxologies, prayers, and blessings continued interminably while my Austrian and Canadian colleagues, both of rotund build, began to look like Madame Tussaud diplomats who had been forgotten in the sun. At last it seemed the service was nearing its end. But no. A Muslim hajji was then called upon to extol the president's virtues to Allah and seek his blessing for the president's continued reign. This was then translated by an interpreter into English, the highlight was the hajji's stated entreaty to Allah to grant the president another 150 years' life. As the sun slowly sank behind the stained glass window over the altar, the light produced a curious but apt effect. In the changing light even Christ looked tired and appeared to be mopping his brow.

The protocol, so elaborate on paper, was in practice related mainly to dress. To be sartorially correct one needed to wear white tie and tails (twice, including once in the streets at midday), morning dress with short black coat (once) and grey morning dress (once). Two top hats, one black and one grey, were required. Some unusual variations on these outfits were observed. One short and stocky Liberian with long arms whom I encountered in a black top hat, white tie and long, ill-fitting, tails was wearing baggy striped pants …

The Liberian government was simply not able to cope with the influx of so many representatives. At first I thought Australia should have been represented by a minister. Subsequently I decided the suffering which the minister concerned would have been called upon to endure would have been beyond the call of duty. Those countries who sent ministers gained no advantage. After the president of the Ivory Coast, the U.S. vice-president, the vice-president of Cameroun and the Crown Prince of Ethiopia everybody was treated alphabetically. The Argentinian, Australian and Austrian representatives, although simply special ambassadors, were thus always prominently placed and fared well under this system. Others were less fortunate.

Ghana had sent Commissioner of Police Nunoo who, as a member of the ruling, seven-man national liberation council, was really something more than a minister. Not only did he receive no special attention but he always found himself sitting in frigid silence next to the representatives of Guinea whose government is harbouring Nkrumah and with which Ghana has no relations.

The Speaker of the Zambian national assembly was of course always placed last. After two days of this he had an epileptic fit which was generally thought to have been induced by his rising anger at his treatment. Germany was represented by a count from Bonn, a man of considerable attachment to protocol. Irritating as the lack of proper protocol was to him, he was also called upon to endure a most egregious error in the spelling of his title in the caption of a photograph in the *Liberian Star*, a paper in which less spectacular misprints normally pass unnoticed because they are so common.

One of the causes of our sufferings, apart from the need to wander around the streets of Monrovia in the midday sun in white tie and tails, was traffic congestion. It was intended that cars should move in a determined order from ceremony to ceremony. This in fact never happened. Quite often two lines of cars moving in opposite directions would meet in a one-way street. When this occurred those near side streets would turn into them only to encounter buses or the Liberian army which seemed to be drilling in the middle of the city for the parade the next day. The result was total chaos. The system — or the lack of it — even succeeded in outwitting the U.S. vice-president's zealous security men who were at one stage completely separated from him.

Once, when our own car and several others were being held up at an intersection on the way to a reception by the president for no apparent reason other than that the president might himself pass in five minutes' time, the resulting traffic jam was only unsnarled by the versatile secretary of state himself, J. Rudolf Grimes. His own car held up, and noticing pink fists being shaken from cars with drooping national pennants at two rather stubborn policemen, he took over the direction of the traffic himself sporting, unusually, but appropriately for the occasion, a black topee.

Overheated, stalled and abandoned cars were a common sight as indeed were their overheated, perspiring, and irritated ambassadorial occupants. The Japanese representative, who was stuck in the motionless line of cars going towards the presidential executive mansion two hours after the function he was supposed to attend had started, suddenly noticed that the car carrying the Indonesian representative from the other direction had stopped beside him. Seeing a sudden and unexpected chance to escape the traffic jam, he leapt from his car across into the Indonesian car. Even if Japanese pride may have suffered a little he saved himself the two remaining hours of the five-mile journey to and from the executive mansion which he had commenced. The motorcades were not without their adventures. Once we found ourselves bumper to bumper with the Thai representative's car. Petrol was pouring out of the tank on to the road while the driver endeavoured to light a cigarette, throwing the matches out of the window as he did so. We blew our horn and gesticulated wildly but were probably thought to be suffering form sunstroke because there was no response from the car in front. We thought we might witness a double diplomatic immolation but disaster was averted when the car ran out of petrol half way up the steep hill to the hotel.

If progress in a car with a flag was slow, it was, in a car without one, virtually impossible. The police had instructions to allow only cars flying their flags to pass. My Canadian colleague suffered many mortifications and missed practically every ceremony at which he had come to represent his country as a result of his stern adherence to principle. The Liberian government had undertaken to provide flags for all representatives present. On arrival he discovered that both the flag on the pole at the hotel and the pennant on his car were the old, and not the new, Canadian maple leaf flag. Stoically he refused to allow the old flag to be flown and devotion to the old flag can rarely have caused a diplomat such discomfort. In our own case the pennant for the car was in fact the Red Ensign, which is never flown on land, but on several occasions we simply had to use it to achieve the purpose of our visit to Monrovia, although it was incorrect to do so. I would strongly recommend that the Australian representative at President Tubman's inevitable seventh inauguration, in four years' time, travels with his own pennant.

Another reason for the confusion was the unpunctuality of the president himself. He was half an hour late for his own intercessory service, an hour late for the national parade, and even 45 minutes late for his own inauguration. This latter lapse resulted in his inaugural address being punctuated by the 21-gun salute which commenced, only three minutes late, at 12.03 p.m. After the first few shattering reports (I was told that at the first shot the Guinean representative threw himself under the seat apparently thinking that a coup was about to take place) the president stopped speaking. After 17 guns had been fired, one did not go off and the president, thinking that the salute was over, began again only to be cut short again by the next report. The president was not actually late for his own inaugural banquet but he did succeed in delaying the start by nearly two hours by asking for the seating plan to be changed. This caused another total breakdown in the protocol arrangements and we finally went into dinner at quarter past eleven.

The inaugural banquet was to be the climax of the celebrations. In the time of Louis XIV it would have been an event, but for a poor and underdeveloped country it was bizarre. Fifteen cooks had been sent to Paris months previously for special training. Foodstuffs had been flown in from several countries. The banquet was held in the executive mansion where the president lives, works, and entertains. It is a very large structure which dominates Monrovia and looks like a luxury hotel or office block. It is said to have cost US$30,000,000, or half of the national budget for one year. The cutlery was of gold and glassware was encrusted with gold filigree. At a conservative estimate, each setting could not have cost less than $300 and there were some 200 people at the banquet.

Once seated it was difficult to move, a problem which was emphasised by the illness of the Asantehene (king) of Ashanti. The Asantehene was upset by one course and, apart from sitting immediately in front of the president, he was in one of the more congested corners. What to do? With regal sang-froid he simply stayed where he was and vomited when he needed to into a soup plate. To leave, he explained later to a guest who sat near him, might have been taken as an insult to the president.

Exhausted guests finally left the banquet hall at 2 o'clock in the morning and I felt somewhat sorry for the U.S. vice-president who was to catch a plane only four hours later from an airport 50 miles from the city.

No account of the proceedings would be complete without a brief description of the national 'parade' which was reviewed by the president the following morning. The president, although commander-in-chief of the armed forces, was nearly an hour late. Indeed, some soldiers were eating fruit, with their rifles on the ground. When he did arrive the parade was not called to attention. The president and several of his generals and admirals in uniforms of a type which used to be seen outside London cinemas inspected some but not all of the troops and then came back to take the army salute and the 'march' past. The army, looking like the remnants of a defeated rabble, shambled rather than marched past the president. The uniforms were crumpled, some soldiers were out of step, which was hardly surprising as I noticed several did not have laces in their boots and one, who must have been in considerable discomfort, was wearing two left boots.

All delegates were decorated by order of the president with the Liberian Humane Order of African Redemption. Strange as it may seem in the light of what I have described, this is the highest decoration in the state. The decorations were acquired by representatives in various ways. I do not think that anybody except the Asantehene of Ashanti was actually decorated by the president. (Perhaps his stoic effort at the state banquet had brought him under special notice.) Some of the decorations appeared in hotel pigeonholes, others were dropped into the back seats of the cars of representatives, while some were handed to them by liaison officers. Two were posted and arrived at the hotel by mail. Nothing, however, equals the presentation to the Austrian representative. The Austrian special ambassador, it is said, was under the shower with his bathroom door unlocked. There was a knock at the door and he said that he was under the shower but would be out soon if the person would kindly wait. The door then opened and a Liberian official, saying that he was very busy and could not wait and that he had a decoration for the ambassador which he should wear at the ball that evening, thrust the order into the naked ambassador's wet hand. The Yugoslav ambassador's medal fell off its ribbon at the ball and he was simply supplied with another Order of the African Redemption from a pile which a member of the protocol department apparently had under his table. A number of representatives at the ceremonies had reached the conclusion by the end of the inauguration that they were, in fact, deserving of Liberia's highest order, notwithstanding their reservations about the method by which it was presented.

Credit should be given where it is due. The Ducor Hotel is a good hotel and it coped extremely well with the large influx of foreign representatives. There were, however, some less fortunate people who were not accommodated at the Ducor Hotel and who fared less well. Some escaped with stomach upsets, but others, including my Sudanese colleague, lost most of his clothes. The American reporters who accompanied their vice-president were, perhaps, the least fortunate of all. By the time they arrived there was no accommodation available in Monrovia. With considerable ingenuity the department of information requisitioned and partially repainted in the course of 12 hours the largest of Monrovia's brothels. When the reporters arrived the 'hotel' sign was still wet and it did not take them very long to realise why they could not find the entrance lobby, the dining room and the main lounge and why the 'hotel' had the aroma of a Port Said powder room.

The Liberians were hospitable and friendly. No offence was ever intended and the shortcomings described in this dispatch were due not to ill-will but to a distorted sense of values, to mistaking pomp for dignity, and to inefficiency and lack of organisation. To say the people are friendly is perhaps an understatement. The Liberian national motto is 'The love of liberty brought us here' to which some residents add 'and the liberty of love kept us here'. I had no experience of this myself but one representative from a country in the south-east Asian region risked a possible treason charge by disappearing from the ceremonies on New Year's eve for the next 26 hours with one of the vice-president's daughters.

I believe that the excessive pomp and expense of the

reinauguration of the president, and the preoccupation of the ruling group with its own wealth, prestige and privilege in a society so in need of so much, is a suitable subject for satire.

If I possessed the abrasive wit or cantankerous iconoclasm of a Malcolm Muggeridge I might continue, but it is not my purpose simply to denigrate Liberia. Liberia enjoys a status and exercises an influence in African councils and in the United Nations which is of some importance. This and the country itself deserve a serious study which I shall attempt in a subsequent dispatch.

I have the honor, sir, to be your obedient servant,

R. Woolcott,

High Commissioner

To handle diplomatically the proliferation of countries, many of which were established on the wreckage of the colonial system, governments often use the United Nations as a point of contact with smaller states. Sometimes they give their heads of missions visiting and reporting responsibilities for other states, or they accredit a visiting ambassador to make occasional official trips from headquarters.

When I was high commissioner in Ghana, for example, I had visiting and reporting responsibilities for ten countries in West Africa, from Mauritania to Togo. This region also included Mali, which gave me the opportunity to visit Timbuktu. A photograph of me astride a camel in the main street, taken by my wife, hung in my office in New York. During a visit, the foreign minister was drawn to the photograph and was obviously keen to visit such an exotic and unusual place himself. On his return to Canberra he asked the department to come up with some reasons why the foreign minister of Australia should visit Timbuktu. In those days, frank and fearless advice was still tended to ministers, and the head of the Africa section responded to the minister's note, 'There are no reasons why you should visit Mali.'

As an experiment, the British foreign office based several of its ambassadors — particularly to some smaller countries — at their headquarters in London. One such appointment has left us with a delightful account of his presentation of credentials to the president of Chad:

> Sir,
>
> I have the honour to report that last Monday I was, as usual at my desk in the Foreign and Commonwealth office. But on Tuesday I flew to Fort Lamy in Chad, 3000 miles away in the middle of Africa, taking with me hastily prepared credentials, a speech and a morning coat. On Wednesday I called on the Chadian Minister of Foreign Affairs, the chief foreign representatives in Fort Lamy and the United Nations representative. On Thursday morning I presented

my credentials to the President and, just over an hour later, flew back to Europe. On Friday I was again back at my desk in the office.

To me therefore fell the honour and privilege of being the first member of the British Diplomatic Service to be appointed as one of Her Majesty's Ambassadors while continuing to serve as Head of a Department in the Foreign and Commonwealth Office. This is an experiment and, as such, it has taken most people by surprise. It is a new departure, reported by one newspaper under the appropriate headline, 'Our man in Chad, isn't'. It is too soon to say whether the arrangement is a practical, sensible and economical one, but I shall do my best to make it so.

He goes on to say that while the Chad government had pressed for the urgent appointment of an ambassador and had argued that he should present credentials on 20 July:

I rashly assumed that I should be given on arrival a program of calls and a firm appointment at the palace. I was indeed met by the Chief of Protocol, but it soon emerged that he had made no plans at all, and that we had to start from scratch; a great deal of tactful prodding of Chadian bureaucracy was required.

Next morning I saw the Minister for Foreign Affairs, M. Baroum, who was on holiday but came into the office specially to receive me.

By the evening, however, we were still without news of any appointment with the President. I was told by my new colleagues, that I might be summoned at five minutes' notice, or alternatively that I might have to wait for several weeks — a prospect that filled me with alarm. More prodding took place, but the lamp of hope burnt low. That night, however, a message came that I was to present my credentials at 10am next day and I retired to bed in a mood of unreasoning euphoria.

On Thursday morning the timing began to slip. The Chief of Protocol rang to say that the time was now to be 10.30 and that he would fetch me at 10.15 or 10.20. A motorcycle escort arrived, the commander of which came up to my room and asked if I could tell him where we were going. I said I thought the President's Palace, but that it was scarcely for me to say. At 10.15, I was on the steps of my hotel in a morning coat. 10.20 passed, then 10.30. No car appeared, the motorcycle escort departed. Time passed. A herd of long-horned cattle were driven by. It began to rain. The little group on the hotel steps settled down into a torpid state. 10.40, 10.45 passed. My return flight was at 12.35. I surrendered to a feeling of despair. There was no more we could do. The rain had stopped, but Africa, and Chad seemed to have won.

Then, astonishingly, the escort reappeared with a car bringing the chief of protocol who explained the delay as due to the shower. Proudly, the chauffeur pressed a button and the car roof opened. My flag (which, luckily, I had remembered to bring out from London) was fixed to the wing, and we set out. All seemed splendid again. Being driven slowly through the streets of Fort Lamy, past the acacias and oleanders, escorted by motorcycles, with even French officers having to salute and a cheer from some Nigerian students at the sight of the British flag, I again thought that our troubles were at an end. But optimism is always premature in Africa. At that point the heavens opened in a cloudburst worthy of the tropics. The rain descended in a solid sheet. The chauffeur prodded a button, but the roof refused to close again. The Chief of Protocol wrung his hands and exclaimed, 'ooh la la' any number of times. Through the deluge, I sought to assure him that he must think nothing of it and that, as an Englishman, I was entirely used to wettings.

I arrived therefore at the palace, through a double line of guards in red and blue with drawn sabres, in the condition of a sponge, with a steaming morning coat, a smell of wet serge, and water running off both elbows. The Chief of Protocol made ineffectual attempts to dry me with a handkerchief. So I advanced and delivered my speech under the klieg lights while the cameras whirred. The President stood motionless with a rigid and forbidding expression on his face. I thought at the time that he was seeking to make an impression of dignity, strength and independence, but on reflection I think he was probably determined not to be the first to burst out laughing at the spectacle of this bedraggled Ambassador emerging like a newt from the waters and proceeding to declaim a formal address. He replied to my speech in very much the same terms as my own — indeed I thought I recognised some phrases out of mine, conveniently appropriated, no doubt, by those who had had to draft the reply. I then handed him my credentials and the ceremony was over.

I have the honour to be, Sir,

Your obedient Servant

In another British dispatch, the ambassador was describing a visit he had made to a province in southern Italy that had been seriously affected by prolonged drought. He reported that the drought was so severe that several of the monks, despite their vows of self-sufficiency and isolation, had come down from their hilltop monastery to buy food from the village in the valley below.

The ambassador's typist, however, had made an egregious error in the dispatch which went unnoticed at the embassy but enjoyed wide circulation at the Foreign Office. Instead of typing the monks had violated their 'holy vows' she had typed they had violated their 'holy cows'. The then foreign secretary, Sir Anthony Eden, who was said, perhaps unfairly, to lack a sense of humour, noted in the margin, 'It seems a Papal Bull is required.'

Australian-born Scot Sir Archibald Clerk Kerr had an extraordinary diplomatic career which included an influential tenure as British ambassador to the Soviet Union during the darkest days of World War II. His wit is famously captured in a delightful, if slightly sad, letter — still held in the British archives — written from Moscow in 1943 to the head of the foreign office, Lord Pembroke.

> My Dear Reggie,
> In these dark days, man tends to look for little shafts of light that spill from Heaven. My days are probably darker than yours, and I need, my God I do, all the light I can get. But I am a decent fellow, and I do not want to be mean and selfish about what little brightness is shed upon me from time to time. So I propose to share with you a tiny flash that has illuminated my sombre life and tell you that God has given me a new Turkish colleague whose card tells me that he is called Mustapha Kunt.
>
> We all feel like that, Reggie, now and then, especially when Spring is upon us, but few of us would care to put it on our cards. It takes a Turk to do that.
>
> Sir Archibald Clerk Kerr
> H.M. Ambassador

Increasingly diplomacy involves public speaking. Usually, this is undertaken to outline Australia's policies and interests, though occasionally a head of mission has the opportunity to address an audience that hopes to be entertained. I was asked to address a jovial annual dinner of the St. Andrews Society in Indonesia. Unknown to me the address was being tape-recorded and so — fortunately or unfortunately — a text of this hardly diplomatic address exists.

Distinguished Chieftain of the Hallowed Society of St. Andrew of Java, highlanders, lowlanders, Calvinists, men of thrift, whisky drinkers, oatcake makers, caber tossers, haggis eaters — to digress for a minute of the subject of haggis, it is well known that several years ago a country, to the anger of the Scots there, banned the import of haggis as a food. However, when you wily countrymen reclassified haggis as a fertiliser its import was permitted — clansmen, Scotsmen, Scotswomen, distinguished guests, and ladies and gentlemen.

My wife and I are honoured to be your guests and I, particularly, am honoured to have the opportunity to speak on behalf of your many guests here tonight. I think it is appropriate that I should be here tonight. I have only a few hours ago returned from a visit to the highlands … of Irian Jaya. This is not as irrelevant as you may think. I found some similarities between the highlands of Scotland and the highlands of Irian Jaya. Firstly, there was much mist and drizzle. Secondly, in their social system they call their clans, tribes. Thirdly, when in the highlands — of Irian Jaya — I encountered a remarkable item of clothing worn by highland men. It is known as a koteka and is, I presume, designed to keep an important part of the highland male warm. It serves, I imagine, a similar purpose in some respects to the Scottish sporran.

Speaking of sporrans reminds me of a young female friend of mine who was asked some years ago in Australia on a radio quiz, 'What is a sporran?' Quite a large prize was at stake. The young lady was puzzled, reflected for a moment and then replied in all innocence 'isn't it the hairy thing which hangs down between a Scotsman's legs'. 'Give the young lady the money', exclaimed the announcer, who was later suspended by his somewhat puritanical station management.

I am somewhat unsure of my credentials to address such an august body as the Java St. Andrew's Society. I must confess my wife, too, had some reservations about coming here tonight, which have been rapidly dispelled by the warmth of your welcome. She is of Danish origin and an ardent feminist, and her earlier reservations related to charges that Scotland's John Knox ranks high amongst the world's MCPs — for those with Malaysian connections, I refer not to the Malaysian Communist Party, but to male chauvinist pigs.

On my own part I am, as I said, uncertain of my credentials. At boarding school I was a secret admirer of the verse of Robbie Burns and the proud possessor of his then banned in Australia, 'Merry Muses — Not for Maids, Ministers, or Striplings'. But despite this, and being a strong chorister in renditions of 'The Ball of Kerrymuir', I must confess that I have never tossed a caber, nor worn a kilt. I must admit to being quite inept at the reel. My appetite for the haggis is only slightly ahead of my appetite for the durian. I do confess, however, to have made one visit to your country that I shall touch on later, and to have allowed an occasional drop of your country's most famous export — other than its proud and friendly people — to pass my lips. Regrettably, I can claim only one Scottish ancestor — a Thwaites on my mother's side who came to Australia early in the 19th century, after an obligatory delay in an English institution for reasons which that side of the family have never fully explained to me. No doubt for some honourable offence such as poaching a salmon or plucking a sleeping laird's sporran.

I referred briefly to my visit to Scotland. This was in 1949 and my overriding memory of that visit is the perfect spring weather — for ducks — and the overwhelming availability of alcohol, in the Edinburgh railway station but not in our hotel, which seemed to be subject to a draconian form of prohibition in 1949. It was May, and a friend and I had journeyed north to play in a Scottish open tennis tournament at Edinburgh. We had been told that the tournament was always held in May because of the reliability of the weather during that month. Well, for three days not a ball was struck, and my partner and I got onto the court only once to push our thumbs into the sodden clay to confirm the abandonment of the tournament. Much of our time was spent in the nearby Edinburgh railway station which proved to be a tolerant and hospitable watering hole. I never did discover if trains left from there.

However, what I may lack in direct connections with Scotland is, I believe, made up for by my sincere respect for what Scotland — sometimes known as the knuckle-end of the British Isles — has contributed to Australia, and indeed to the world. The Scots are a proud, determined, and resourceful people and Australia owes much of its rapid progress, in its relatively short span of national life, to many able Scottish immigrants. Australian history is studded with famous Scots who have made a significant contribution, perhaps the best known of whom is our longest serving prime minister and Knight of the Thistle, Sir Robert Gordon Menzies — or Mingies as I believe it would be pronounced in Scotland — with whom I have had the pleasure of working.

Another famous Scot is a former lord mayor of Perth — a city whose very name is derived from Scotland — Sir Harry Howard. Sir Harry was a true Scot with a strong Scottish accent, despite his many years in Australia and his un-Scottish sounding name. Dare I tell you the tale of Sir Harry? I hesitate because the British diarist, Lady Holland, once wrote, 'it requires a surgical operation to get a joke well into a Scotsman's understanding'. From my own experience I find this quite false. So if I may, I shall consign diplomatic discretion to the wind for a moment and tell the true tale of Sir Harry.

Some years ago, the famous Antarctic explorer and scientist, Sir Vivian Fuchs, visited Perth — the Australian Perth — and was to be given the key of that gracious city at a mayoral reception by Sir Harry. Addressing the large gathering in the Perth town hall Sir Harry said, 'It is a very great pleasure for we citizens of Perth to have with us tonight the distinguished Antarctic explorer Sir Vivian Fucks'. Sir Vivian, blushing, lent forward and tugged Sir Harry's sleeve, 'Mr Mayor, its pronounced Fooks'. Sir Harry turned and said, 'Aye, but I n'er could say that in public'.

Apart from Sir Robert and Sir Harry, I should mention that our present prime minister, Malcolm Fraser, is also of Scottish origin. What better man to head the government of financial restraint than a man who has inherited the virtue of thrift from his ancestors.

In your chieftain's speech he made some reference to Scottish separatism. I do not know how many of you study here the *Antara* news bulletin, but it is part of my job to do so, and a most timely item appeared this morning. Scotland's separatists have found a new champion. According to this morning's *Antara*, President Idi Amin of Uganda has described himself as the 'uncrowned king of

Scotland' and said he will personally attend the celebration of that country's independence from the United Kingdom. Moreover, according to the report, the Ugandan president has even offered to send pipers from Uganda to entertain the Scottish people. I am far from sure that Scots would regard President Amin as a truly appropriate heir of Bonnie Prince Charlie in some future restored Scottish monarchy. But I felt obliged to draw the attention of the Java St. Andrew's Society to this interesting and indeed timely Antara report this morning.

Not surprisingly at this hour of the night, you seem a most responsive audience and I might be permitted one final joke. A Scotsman lay dying and had his best friend called to his bedside. His friend asked, 'Is there any last wish which I can fulfil for you, Jock?' 'Yes, there is Mac', the dying man said. 'As a mark of our mutual respect for our whisky, I would count it an honour if you would pour a bottle of Scotch whisky over my grave once a week.' The friend pondered this for a minute and then replied, 'Aye, I'll do it, but you won't mind if I pass it through my kidneys first.'

And so, to turn from such grave matters (laughter) to tonight's lively realities. chieftain, distinguished guests, ladies and gentlemen, I would like to salute those Scots in Indonesia who have gathered here to celebrate St. Andrew's day. I would like to thank you once again for inviting my wife and me to be with you in this friendly and jovial atmosphere. And, finally, on behalf of the guests here tonight, I would like to propose a toast to the Java St. Andrew Society, and to the proud, imaginative and adventurous people which the society represents.

Ladies and Gentlemen — our generous Hosts.

Thank you.

CHAPTER 5

One liver and one stomach to give for one's country

Food comes first, then morals. — Bertolt Brecht

What is usually referred to in diplomatic parlance as representational activity — entertaining, eating, and drinking — has often lubricated the wheels of diplomacy, especially during the negotiating process. In his book, *Australian Ambassador* (1979), Walter Crocker acknowledged the considerable strain on the diplomat's digestive system by aptly naming the second chapter, 'Three Thousand Cocktail Parties for my Country'.

I had the dubious honour of being quoted in the *New York Times* as saying that the qualities required for a

'A sound mind, a good tailor, and a strong liver.'

successful ambassador to the United Nations were, amongst others, 'a sound mind, a good tailor, and a strong liver'. As the number of sovereign states increases so too do the number of receptions, and the strain imposed on the ambassador's one and only liver. While in New York, I regarded receptions as working events at which one could explain a policy issue or secure a vote, thereby saving several official calls. Nevertheless, I often felt that the cost of some of these receptions could feed a village in Somalia or Bangladesh for a month.

Vodka to the Russians, like maotai to the Chinese, is not just a drink — it is more a way of life. When Mikhail Gorbachev became secretary general of the Communist Party, he moved to reduce excessive vodka consumption by increasing its price and extolling the virtues of tomato juice. Needless to say, this was very unpopular. Tomato juice in Russian is called *tomatne cok,* and Gorbachev's title was usually abbreviated to *Cekgen,* so wits around Moscow bars started referring to him as the *Cokgen* — the juice general.

I had heard about the strength of maotai before I visited China. A retired English civil servant in Burma who had spent several years near the Burma/China border told me that he had found maotai to be very useful: it was an excellent polish for the buttons on his colonial tunic, and in the evenings it proved to be an effective insect repellent. But, he added, 'I never drank the stuff.'

I first sampled maotai at a banquet in the Great Hall of the People during the first Australian prime ministerial visit to China with Gough Whitlam. Two members of the prime minister's staff, well known around Canberra's watering holes for their prodigious capacity, stole the show. Maotai containers aptly resembled Australian Brasso cans, a popular metal polish. To the amazement of the Chinese at our table they each consumed a whole container and, although flushed and perspiring profusely they remained on their feet. Hearing on the grapevine of the two Australians' heroic performance, no less a person than Chou En Lai, the Chinese premier, came to shake hands with the two visitors who had performed such a feat!

Provincial travel in the Philippines usually involved a ritual feast of barbequed pig, what the locals call lechón. After a number of such feasts on official tours, embassy wits prepared the following recipe:

Ingredients

1 pig (lechón)

1 bucket of old grass clipppings and banana leaves

inestimable quantities of San Miguel beer

Implements

1 blunt razor

1 x 10 foot bamboo pole, sharpened at one end

1 fire with spit supports

1 very sharp bolo

Method

First steal your pig. This may be difficult if ambassador Woolcott's convoy has just passed by as most pigs, together with chooks, dogs, and other inoffensive livestock will have been run over.

Take the blunt razor and shave the pig roughly, making sure not to cut off more than 50 per cent of the hair.

Take the bucketful of grass cuttings and banana leaves and, using an ungloved hand, stuff the pig full.

Take the bamboo pole and pass through the pig, from south to north, sharp end first, leaving an equal length of pole protruding from each orifice.

Then kill the pig.

> Now suspend the pig on the spit supports over a charcoal and dung fire. Turn the pig on the spit at irrregular intervals until it is about half cooked.
>
> Remove the pig from the fire and stand it, on its pole, against a wall, in the sun, to cool.
>
> When it is almost cold, take a very sharp bolo and, using the reverse edge, ceremoniously remove the lechón's nose, ears, and other protuberances.
>
> Cut the lechón into two-inch cubes and separate the pieces into two heaps, one comprising pieces containing bone, and the other pieces which are bone free.
>
> Discard the bone-free pieces, and leave the others in a place in which they are likely to gather flies.
>
> Serve amid chaos with warm San Miguel beer.
>
> Serves from one person to a battalion.

Lady Tange's 65-page *Notes for Wives of Officers of the Department of Foreign Affairs* devoted seven pages to 'relations with servants', and raised some hackles in egalitarian Australia where servants are an unusual luxury. The book also offered advice on such matters as what to do if, at an official function, you were offered something you simply could not eat or drink, such as *koumis* (fermented mare's milk) in Central Asia, camel's penis in Oman, or bear's paws in China. My wife once surreptitiously filled her handbag with blubbery sea-cucumbers to avoid displeasing her senior Chinese host, only to be given a second serving of these slugs — claimed by coastal Chinese to be a potent aphrodisiac — when her plate was seen to be empty.

While we are on the subject of controversial foods, there is a tale of an ecumenical gathering in Rome at which representatives of the major religions were present. At the evening reception, the unfathomably-named 'devils on horseback' — prunes wrapped in bacon — were being served. A Catholic priest offered one to a mufti standing nearby, 'You should try one of these; they are very tasty'. Surprised, the mufti replied, 'No, thank you. You must know it is against my religion to eat bacon.' Later that evening when the mufti was taking his leave he said to the priest, 'I am sorry I did not meet your wife.' The priest, rather taken aback, replied, 'I am not married. I am celibate.' The mufti smiled and said, 'I am sorry. I forgot. But you might try it sometime. It's better than bacon.' Payback time.

The official lunch/dinner/reception round can be challenging and often boring, but diplomatic life overseas does have its gastronomic delights and delicacies too. In Moscow, we often ate black caviar from the Caspian Sea, sometimes even for breakfast in the days when it was both cheap and available; in China we ate Peking duck, and caneton a l'orange in France; paella in Spain; and at Simpsons on the Strand in London, the traditional roast beef and Yorkshire pudding. One of my predecessors at the

embassy in Ghana was a mango lover and he used to send his driver to Ouagadugu, the capital of Upper Volta (now Burkina Faso), a journey of some 400 kilometres, to buy the fruit for his official dinners.

The fascinating island of Ternate lies just off the orchid-shaped island of Halmahera, situated between Menado in North Sulawesi and the parrot's beak at the western end of West Papua. It was here that I discovered a very special delicacy — coconut crabs. These enormous crabs come ashore in the evening, climb the coconut trees at the edge of the sea and with their large and powerful right claws — which can snap a broom stick — sever the coconut so that it falls ten metres to the ground. They then use their claws to break open the coconut to get at the white flesh within.

We decided we should take some of these exotic delights back to Jakarta on our DC-3. For a small sum, several experienced locals captured three crabs for us and placed the large creatures in a plywood box with the lid lightly nailed down. The DC-3's crew were concerned about where the box should be stowed. The baggage hold was ruled out as too cold and so we reluctantly decided to forgo the comfort of the toilet in the tail of the aircraft and placed the box there. As an additional precaution a crewman wrapped wire around the box.

Once airborne we could hear even through the toilet door the angry beasts trying to break out of their prison. To his horror, when one of the crew opened the door to see what the noise was all about, he faced an enormous claw snapping the air. We should have realised that for a creature that could split open a coconut a plywood box would hardly hold three of them for long. What should we do? We could hardly face the prospect of the enraged crabs loose in the toilet or, worse still, in the body of the aircraft. A crew member tried to force the offending claw back into the box with a broom, only to have the handle snapped in two. He eventually succeeded with a metal lever from the aircraft tool kit, and additional wire was wound around the box.

When we arrived in Jakarta with the case still shaking

from the angry crabs inside it was conveyed to the official residence. I told the cook we had some large, special, and very tasty crabs to be cooked as we were inviting a few friends for dinner. She had never heard of coconut crabs or of their reputation, and when she cut the wires of the box the lid flew off and a large crab landed on the kitchen floor. When it moved menacingly towards her, the cook screamed, grabbed a broom and thrust it at the massive claw which snapped the handle as if it was a match.

I came to the rescue with a steel handled broom which the crab dented but could not break. In tears, our cook said she could not cope and suggested that my deputy's cook, who came from the Philippines, should come and help her. Eventually, we removed the three creatures into a large pot of boiling water.

That evening we had a superb feast. As one guest said, the experience of fresh, soft, succulent crabmeat infused with coconut flavour was something he would never forget — nor shall I.

CHAPTER 6

Official tourism

For lust of knowing what should not be known, we make the golden journey to Samarkand.
— James Elroy Flecker

Diplomacy involves a great deal of travel, usually on duty, but occasionally, I dare to admit, it is tourism under the cloak of official activity. Bali is an idyllic island of great beauty that Jawaharlal Nehru once described as the 'morning of the world'. To avoid suspicion in Canberra that my visits there were a form of official tourism — which would of course have been quite baseless — I avoided using the name Bali in my cables, preferring to report that I was visiting Den Pasar, the island's capital. In the course of my career I have undertaken 'official' travel by car, by air, by rail, by sea, by river, by helicopter, on foot, on horseback, by camel, and on occasions by combinations of these methods.

Diplomats are often envied because they travel the world and mix with interesting people. While there are such advantages, not all posts are pleasant, comfortable, and healthy, or places to which one would want to travel by choice. I recall a British colleague in Moscow being delighted to have received a telegram from the foreign office suggesting a posting to Italy. He did not enjoy Moscow and was eager to accept Rome, and so that evening we had few drinks to celebrate. The next day he contacted me. He was desolate. He had received a second telegram stating that the first had been mutilated in transit and that Rome should have read Lomé; the small capital of Togo in West Africa was not quite what he had hoped for.

Diplomatic travellers are, as a rule, more concerned about travel by road or air than in lifts, but a notice in a lift in an old building in Rome gave me pause for thought. It advised passengers on 'How to survive in a plummeting elevator', urging them not to panic but to 'flatten your body against the car floor when the elevator begins to plummet uncontrollably'. The note also offered the calming thoughts that 'there have been very few recorded incidents involving death' in elevators.

Sadly, a number of my colleagues have died in plane

crashes. Because of its impeccable safety record, I flew Qantas whenever possible. Despite close calls in dubious carriers such as Aeroflot in the 1950s, Air Mali, and Royal Air Lao, I somehow survived. If, like the proverbial cat, a diplomat has nine lives, I have doubtless spent several of them in the service of my country. I was once sitting beside a lady flying across the Tasman in rough weather. She seemed nervous and was fingering a cross hanging from her neck. Hoping to relax her, I said, 'You are not afraid of flying are you?' 'No', she replied with impeccable logic, 'but I am afraid of crashing.'

Some years ago my wife and I were arrested in East Africa when our pilot landed at the wrong airport in Mozambique. It was during the cold war, and it took some time and diplomacy to explain to our leftist captors that we were not spies and that it was a genuine pilot error. Once, on an Aeroflot jet, we were diverted to Omsk in foul weather. Looking out of the window as we descended through heavy rain, I was shocked to see not far from our wingtip a large concrete chimneystack looming up out of the clouds. We missed it, but I admit I was still trembling when we hit the runway rather hard a few seconds later.

While in an Australian naval helicopter flying low over Sarawak during Indonesia's military action against the establishment of Malaysia, a bullet passed through the compartment, luckily without hitting any of the occupants.

While taking off in a seaplane from the lake at the site of the major International Nickel Corporation (INCO) mine in Sulawesi, it stalled and fell back heavily into the water. An Air Mali flight my wife and I took from Accra to Bamako crashed with the loss of all on board, including some goats, on the return journey. We fortunately had arranged to return by Land Rover.

Despite these misadventures, my career has taken me from Argentina to Antarctica, from Botswana to Bermuda, from Cambodia to Cuba, from Denmark to Djibouti, from Egypt to Eritrea, from Fiji to Finland, from Indonesia to India, in fact virtually all through the alphabet to Zanzibar and Zimbabwe. Indeed, it has taken me to such exotic destinations as Samarkand in Central Asia, Timbuktu, the three gorges on the Yangtze river before they were lost, West Papua, and Antarctica.

I have also been to all 26 provinces of Indonesia, all the provinces of the Philippines, and every state of Malaysia. Much of this official travel around the archipelagos was easily accomplished in the 1970s and 1980s because one of the great privileges enjoyed by an Australian ambassador to these countries was the use of a reliable, if ancient, DC-3 operated by redoubtable members of the Australian air force transport command based in Butterworth in Malaysia.

Staff of the embassy rudely referred to the plane as 'the

blue streak', the flying 'African queen', or 'Kangaroo One', and irreverently called these tours 'ego trips' or 'Monty Woolcott's flying circus'. While they were invaluable in widening our knowledge of these countries of importance to Australia and in extending our contacts, they were also good fun and had their amusing moments.

Apart from the official duties we also had our scary incidents. We landed during a fierce storm in Ujung Pandang in Sulawesi. It turned into a typhoon and the DC-3 had to be anchored to a steamroller. The city was flooded for two days before we could return to the airport. On another occasion, we landed at Basco on Batanes, the northernmost island of the Philippines. The grass runway turned out to be shorter than that recorded in the RAAF handbook and it sloped so sharply that we could only land uphill. The downhill take-off meant dropping off the cliff edge above the sea, an experience our pilot said he would not want to repeat without the benefit of tranquilisers. Our captain made sure that the RAAF handbook was amended on his return to Butterworth.

Despite occasional undiplomatic incidents, these travels generated a surprising amount of favourable publicity for Australia in both Indonesia and the Philippines. On one occasion, giving our spare seat to a leading regional journalist for a flight to Iloilo resulted in a full-page report in the major provincial newspaper. In Australia this might be called 'cash for comment' — although no cash changed hands, and no comment was sought — but it paid handsome dividends.

> What was it like in the Ambassador's plane? Well it was a bit of Australia up in the sky. Everything definitely was Australian — the atmosphere, conversation, jokes, accent, people, refreshments, (preceded by perfumed, moist hand and pink face towels), candies, soft drinks, and Anchor beer. The attention of the cummerbanded handsome steward in a white long-sleeved shirt was truly one for royalty, and one felt like a royal with service *de luxe*.
>
> Tall Denmark-born fashionplate blonde ambassadress Birgit Woolcott, who always looked like she had just stepped out of *Vogue* or *Harpers Bazaar* magazine pages was always an inspiration …

Modesty — or honesty, actually — prohibits me from repeating his words about me and other members of the embassy staff. One wonders what superlatives he could have found to describe a free first-class flight on Qantas or Singapore Airlines.

Our daughter Anna accompanied us on several tours around the Philippines. My deputy nicknamed her 'Hilda' because so many of the introductions in various townships began by welcoming my wife, the ambassador, and 'his lovely daughter Anna'.

A flight on Royal Air Lao led me to send the following official note of warning to my department in 1974:

> Unless the situation has changed appeciably in the last fortnight I would strongly recommend that our officers and couriers be discouraged from using Royal Air Lao flights between Bangkok and Vientiane.
>
> After considerable uncertainty about whether the aircraft would go at all on the evening on which Mr Williams and I took the RAL flight, we were finally rushed to the airport to find a 42-year-old Boeing 307 awaiting us. I am told that this is the last such aircaft in existence, the other 11 having crashed. Its rightful place is in the Smithsonian Institute as a musem piece. The aircraft had in fact been freshly repainted and did not look quite as antiquated in the evening light as it was. I understand that it had been purchased by a Chinese businessman from Flying Tiger Airlines some years ago.
>
> The pilot, 'Captain' Liu, has had his licence withdrawn, even in Cambodia where he recently had the most recent of his 8 crashes. One could argue that, given his experience and the fact that his wings are not yet 'forever folded', he could well be good man in a crisis. Somewhat more remarkable, however, is the fact that his 'co-pilot' is in fact a mechanic and has no licence at all. I understand that while he can take

an aircraft off and make a straight landing he cannot bank it. He also crashed a DC-3 recently in Cambodia, although this feat still places him well behind his captain.

During the flight from Bangkok to Vientiane I noticed the red port wing light went out. What I was unaware of, however, until after the flight was that all the instrument lights in the cockpit had also gone out. As we were making an instrument landing at night the co-pilot had to hold a torch above the instrument panel. Despite this we arrived in one piece, the aged 307 shuddering to a stop at the end of the runway, Captain Liu having landed more than half way down its length.

In case you think I may be exercising some diplomatic licence or exaggeration in describing this remarkable flight, ponder the following. When we returned from Nong Kai, on the Thai side of the Thai/Lao border, to Bangkok we did so on the overnight train — an alternative I would recommend to other travellers of this exotic route. Apart from the fact that the train is comfortable and air-conditioned, the more adventurous traveller can avail himself of a service unusual even in an unsually hospitable country. It is possible to reserve at the station a single sleeper or a double sleeper, the latter with or without a companion for whom payment can be made at the ticket office as part of the fare. But the real point of this part of my report is that we met on the train the Austrian who manages the Royal Air Lao airport restaurant in Vientiane. He said that although he had free travel at any time he chose on Royal Air Lao, he preferred to take the train at considerable personal expense. We also discovered on the train a number of Americans from the embassy in Vientiane who said they had been told not to fly Royal Air Lao.

I think that, in the circumstances, we would be well advised to warn our own officers and their families to use the Thai International flight, which goes once a week, or the train, whether or not they wish to avail themselves of the unnusual services provided buy the latter mode of travel.

Richard Woolcott

Deputy Secretary

In my extensive travels, I have stayed in many grand hotels. When I accompanied Robert Menzies as an advisor on his last official visit to the United Kingdom we stayed at the Savoy in London. But more often than not, I made do with less salubrious accommodation. In the diplomatic profession one needs to be able to feel equally at home in Buckingham Palace or the White House or in some hovel in a remote area. I have spent nights in a rat-infested room with an earth floor through which ran an open drain. My wife and I were once accommodated in the Malian desert in a mudbrick 'hotel' where we were wakened at 4.00 a.m. to a crescendo of braying to discover that we were situated right next to a donkey market.

Australia had a major aid project in Zamboanga del Sur in the Philippines that I was obliged to visit every few months to check on progress and security issues. I usually stayed at the project campsite. After my second visit, I received a touching letter from the manager of a small hotel in Pagadian inviting me to stay at his hotel when I was next in the area. He noted with some pride that, following an inspection by the Department of Tourism in Manila, his establishment had been 'upgraded to a one-star hotel'. I accepted his kind invitation, but sadly, before my next trip, the hotel caught fire due to faulty electrical wiring and was burnt to the ground.

In their travels, ambassadors are invited to do many things, sometimes to raise the profile of a local event. I have committed awful sins of song and dance in the service of my country. On a number of occasions I have been asked to judge beauty contests, and twice I was foolish enough to accept. While on a panel of six judging the Miss Manila contest the judge on my left was the agriculture minister, and he had a clear favourite. He whispered to me, 'Vote for number eleven. She is going places — for starters, to my place.' He invited me to a party that night and, while discretion got the better of curiosity, I understand the winner — number eleven — was there.

The other occasion was a provincial contest in West Africa. As a foreign dignitary, I was invited to introduce the proceedings in what appeared to be a cattle yard. As I concluded my stirring remarks there were cries of 'xasunga, xasunga' from a group of jovial men in the crowd. As the mayor led me out of the yard to where the beauty contestants were lined up, he steered me past some droppings warning, 'don't step in the xasunga'. Just as the moment of judgement arrived there was a power failure. Undeterred, the mayor provided me and the other two judges with kerosene lamps. Judging faces on a dark night in such lighting is hardly conducive to clear results.

But this was only the beginning of my difficulties. One of the girls alleged that the other two judges were intimate friends of the girls who had been placed first and second. She shouted that only I, the foreigner, could be a truly impartial judge, and that she believed I would judge her the winner. This situation taxed my diplomatic skills. I suggested that, in the interests of fairness, the contest should be rejudged the following evening under electric light at the mayor's residence which had a generator. I added that, with enormous regret, I personally would not be able to make the judgement as I had to return to the capital early next morning.

CHAPTER 7

Security and intelligence

The whole aim of politics is to keep the populace alarmed — and hence clamorous to be led to safety.
— H.L. Mencken

I find it a distasteful reality that the politics of fear is much in vogue with incumbent governments — especially in Australia, America, and Britain. If you can keep the people on edge and concerned about real or imagined terrorist threats, they will be reluctant to change governments. But security, espionage, and intelligence activities have always been the handmaidens of diplomacy, though shrouded in mystery. I recall on a school visit an innocent student who thought a 'KGB plant' was some kind of flora.

My first serious encounter with a security situation was when the staff of the Australian embassy in Moscow were given 24 hours' notice to leave the Soviet Union. Our chargé d'affaires ordered me and another third secretary to destroy all our secret documents. Uncertain about what to do in the limited time we had, we took boxes of classified files and cipher books down to the basement and started throwing them into the embassy's furnace.

After about an hour there was a loud beating on the locked door. We opened it slightly to find a frantic Pyotr, the boiler attendant, who told us that the chargé d'affaires had narrowly avoided being hit by a jet of steam when he tried to take a shower on the second floor. Pyotr was not literate and therefore unlikely to see any important secrets, so we let him in. Wide-eyed, he pointed to the pressure gauge at the top of the boiler; the needle had entered the red section, indicating overheating. We told him not to worry, because the needle was not yet at the dangerous end of the red zone. He rolled his eyes as though we were mad and shouted in Russian, 'But it's on the second time around!'

I was surprised when I arrived in Moscow on my first diplomatic posting to discover that the then British ambassador, Sir Alvery Gasgoine, a traditional British aristocrat, was deaf — a considerable disability in groups that exchanged views on the Soviet Union in whispers for fear of eavesdroppers. Sir Alvery was the only real person I have ever known who actually had an ear trumpet into which you were expected to speak when addressing him.

The British embassy was 'swept' annually by a team from MI6 in order to detect and deactivate any listening devices that may have been planted by Soviet intelligence. The most famous of these recording devices was found not in the British, but in the American embassy in the beak of a large wooden eagle mounted on the wall above the desk in the ambassador's office.

To protect their real profession from suspicious Soviet officials, members of these British teams entered the Soviet Union under various guises. They were described, somewhat improbably, as ballet dancers or ballet enthusiasts on their visa applications. Although more interested in ice hockey and bars, they dutifully spent some of their evenings at the Bolshoi Theatre watching, as one Sheffield redneck described it, 'poofters prancing around the stage'.

One evening the British sweepers thought their sensitive equipment had picked up something suspicious on the first floor of the embassy residence. They lifted the carpet and started to remove the floorboards in the centre of the room. 'Cop this. We are onto something big here', one of the sweepers said, looking at a sizeable knuckle of red, black, and green wires. When they had uncovered the full extent of the wiring, they started cutting the wires at what appeared to be their entry point. As the last wire was triumphantly cut they

Dropping in on the ambassador's dinner party.

heard a shattering crash below. They had disconnected not the central point of an elaborate listening device, but a large and elegant chandelier above the ambassadorial dining table in the room below. Cut loose, it had crashed onto the mahogany table as the ambassador's surprised guests were about to sit down to dinner!

The ambassador's dining room was the site of an even more absurd intelligence misadventure. An undercover MI6 agent was attending a dinner at which — unusually in those days — two senior Russian defence officials were to be present. The Russian-speaking agent, no doubt for some good, but unimaginable reason, was disguised as a woman. With a blonde wig, false bust, and an elegant black dress he looked the part.

A young British diplomatic officer, a bachelor filling in for a guest who had withdrawn from the dinner and who was unaware of the situation, found himself sitting beside a very attractive 'woman'. Attractive, non-Russian women were in short supply at the British embassy, and, emboldened by alcohol, he put his hand on her knee under the table. After another glass of wine and not meeting any resistance he moved his hand under her dress further along her thigh. The 'lady' suddenly became animated, reached for her handbag, extracted her lipstick and surreptitiously scribbled a note on the back of her place card which she passed to her eager companion, 'When you come to the balls, show no surprise. Ponsonby, MI6'. Ah, the guile of the British secret service.

As we have seen all too clearly in Iraq, intelligence is often speculative and inaccurate. In a classic case in Jakarta, the US government had become aware of rumors that President Sukarno was having weekly kidney and urological tests. A CIA undercover agent was tasked to ascertain the state of health of the increasingly erratic and anti-American president.

Presidential urine is obviously hard to come by, except possibly in India where in the past several leaders have drunk their own urine for health reasons. They were literally 'on the piss' as an Australian journalist once told me during an Indian prime ministerial visit.

The CIA agent and an orderly from the Korle Bu hospital met at a secret nocturnal location where a bottle of urine was exchanged for a handsome reward in US dollars. It was then sent by diplomatic bag to Washington for analysis. On the basis of these tests, the CIA advised the US administration that they need not be concerned about Sukarno's activities — he was suffering from cancer of the kidneys, bladder, and prostate and had no more than five or six months to live. It is unknown from which patient the 'presidential' urine was taken, but Sukarno lived for another eight years!

A well-established technique used by the KGB to subvert foreign male diplomats was to entice them into compromising situations with Soviet female agents which would be clandestinely photographed. The diplomat would be shown the photographs and records of meetings and threatened with exposure unless there was an agreement to cooperate in future with the Soviet authorities. Such blackmail worked on a number of occasions, but not always.

When Ghana opened its embassy in Moscow, I gave the Ghanaian diplomats considerable assistance, having been through the process of reopening the Australian embassy. One member of the Ghanaian staff — a handsome, robust, and single second secretary — found himself summoned to the foreign ministry. Several stern-looking Soviet officials spread a number of explicit photographs on the table. Gravely, they told the young diplomat that, unless he cooperated with the Soviet authorities, the pictures would be sent to his ministry in Accra. To the surprise and chagrin of his interlocutors, the diplomat — unphased — replied, 'That's okay, but could I have two copies of each of pictures one, three, four, and six to share with my friends before you forward them to Accra.'

On another posting in a country where it was the practice to auction airfreighted items that had not been claimed for six months, I was browsing through the weekly government gazette and was surprised to see advertised for sale 'one Bulgarian diplomatic bag'. Perhaps it was purchased by a Bulgarian embassy security officer.

CHAPTER 8
Fancy dress

All styles are good except the tiresome kind.
— Voltaire

Diplomats often find themselves genuflecting before the local community in the hope of being accepted by the country in which they are serving. Such adventures in *haute couture* can either prove to be harmless activities or result in disaster.

In Kromantse, Ghana, I was ritually enstooled. This is not a medical procedure, but the process of being made a chief in West Africa during which one sits on a stool rather than a throne. If a chief abdicates or is removed, he is said to be destooled, which sounds even more medically unpleasant. My enstooling as Nana Adaban II took place in

A ritual enstoolment.

a very colourful ceremony overlooking the Atlantic Ocean near Cape Coast. Three young 'brides' attended me as I was dressed in the magnificent Kente cloth ceremonial robes of the stool. Even at the risk of offending some local custom, I felt I could not accept their services, but I'm sure that these shy, well-dressed young girls were not all that displeased to be spared the attentions of a foreign diplomat.

I was then borne aloft on a palanquin by six strapping young Africans perspiring under a fierce tropical sun and, followed by the population of the town, carried to the top of a hill. My wife and daughter were asked, as local custom demanded, to follow at a 'respectful distance' behind the palanquin, while my younger son, regarded as my 'soul', was carried in a second palanquin as tradition required. He nearly had his head blown off as excited musketeers discharged their ancient blunderbusses into the air.

On the subject of stools and thrones, I was told a tale by a relative of the king of Swaziland, a country which was at one time in my area of diplomatic responsibility. He said that one of the king's sons coveted the throne and, impatient to succeed his father, commissioned an elaborate wooden throne to be carved in secret. When it was completed he had it concealed at night in the grass roof of his house in the royal compound. Some time later, a fierce windstorm struck the compound and the throne crashed onto the son in his bed below, killing him. This led a sagacious Swazi elder to announce, 'There is a moral in this sad event. It is that people who live in grass houses shouldn't stow thrones.'

In Poso, Indonesia, my wife and I were dressed in magnificent robes by six elders of this region of Sulawesi and given the titles of Dago and Dagin Mposo. In Australian slang *dago* used to be a pejorative word for an Italian migrant. When a photograph of the event appeared in the press, an Australian government minister sent me a letter that began with the politically incorrect salutation, 'My dear Dago'.

Our high commissioner in New Delhi, a former academic with a cruel pen, once described the very tall and angular wife of his American colleague who had adopted the practice of wearing loose fitting saris to evening events as resembling 'a camel in a nightgown'.

These relatively harmless events pale, however, when compared with the suggestion advanced by one of my predecessors as secretary of the department, that Australian representatives should have a diplomatic uniform. His idea was that Australian diplomats would, if so attired, cease to be regarded as 'pale imitations' of their British and American colleagues or, worse still, as indistinguishable from their New Zealand counterparts. A number of older and more traditional foreign services do wear uniforms, although some of them are not unlike those worn by doormen at some five-star hotels in Europe.

A uniform was designed after much discussion behind closed doors. Pith helmets and exotic feathers were ruled out, but a cocked hat or an Akubra with corks dangling from the brim were suggested, I suspect in jest. Should we have gold, brass, or silver buttons? And footwear: how about R.M. Williams' elastic-sided boots, with thongs as an alternative in the tropics? The Swedish diplomatic uniform includes a sword; should ours?

It is on record that at the formal reception for the prince of the Netherlands' visit to South Africa, our high commissioner, a crusty and wounded survivor of wartime combat, found himself displaced in the queue to shake the royal hand by his Swedish colleague who was wearing full regalia. Disturbed by the ordinariness of his grey flannel suit, and fuelled by a few pre-reception drinks, he lunged at the Swede's dangling scabbard demanding, 'What did you get this sword for, defending your bloody neutrality?'

The idea of an Australian uniform leaked to the press, which had a field day with headlines such as, 'Wattle they think of next?', 'Our Diplomats in Fancy Dress', and 'Dinkum Diplomats!' The *Sydney Morning Herald* thundered editorially:

> These garments are reputed to be similar to Nehru or Mao suits; single breasted, with high choker collars on which sprigs of wattle will be embroidered in gold

> thread ... [they] arouse deep misgivings. Our diplomats should be neither ugly Australians nor synthetic Australians.

Given the publicity this potential sartorial disaster received, it was consigned to the shredder by Senator Willesee, then foreign minister.

I fear Australian sartorial ingenuity will be put to an unavoidable test when we host the Asia Pacific Economic Cooperation (APEC) Heads of Government meeting in September 2007. Our prime minister will be expected to follow custom and present a distinctive national Australian shirt or garment to the visiting HOGs. This is not difficult for Indonesia or the Philippines with their traditional batik and barong, but it will no doubt pose problems for us.

Perhaps the PM will resolve the matter by settling for an unbuttoned khaki crocodile hunter's shirt, which could also serve a secondary purpose of memorialising Steve Irwin. If the weather is inclement, a long brown Drizabone coat could be a feature, although this could be regarded as payback to the Vietnamese prime minister for having obliged our leader in 2006 to wear a bright blue, ankle-length *ao dai* normally worn by Vietnamese women, and in which — not to mince words — he looked like my great aunt in her long nightrobe.

These colourful practices continue. In September 2006,

Andrew Peacock, our former foreign minister and ambassador, was appointed a Grand Companion of the Order of Logohu by the government of Papua New Guinea. This entitles him to add 'Bird of Paradise' to his list of achievements, although I doubt whether, given his name, he would add to it a further reference to plumage.

As I have noted, diplomats are often depicted wearing colourful sashes and decorations. Many European countries make a practice of awarding decorations to each other's representatives as well as to their own. Queen Victoria once famously refused permission for a British ambassador to receive a European decoration saying, 'My dogs shall not wear foreign collars.' As compensation the queen has traditionally honoured British heads of mission with knighthoods, unless they have been involved in a known scandal of some magnitude.

Australian diplomats — unlike our senior armed service officers and some heads of departments including, I am sad to observe, those from foreign affairs and trade — do not receive awards in the Order of Australia just for carrying out their normal duties. Nor should they. Australian honours should be awarded only for special achievements otherwise the system will become more suspect than it is already.

I should confess that I have been the recipient of two awards in the Order of Australia which, discarding modesty, were for contributions beyond one's normal duties. They were for special activities related to Australia's election to the Security Council in 1984 (the last time we were able to secure election to the Council) with a then record majority, and — in the face of initial scepticism — for securing regional support for the Australian initiative to establish APEC forum in 1989.

I have also been the recipient of several foreign awards. One is a valued order from the Indonesian government, the Bintang Mahaputra Utama, which translates quaintly into the 'star of the first great prince', in recognition of services to bilateral relations and wider regional cooperation, also related to the establishment of APEC. Another, the Order of the African Redemption, I described in the chapter *Your obedient servant*.

In France, related to my duties on the Security Council when it met in Paris, I visited a wine festival and tasting in Lyon and was awarded the *Chevaliers du Taste Vin*, with a red and yellow sash from which hangs a silver drinking vessel. I suspect I received this simply because I was there rather than for my oenological expertise.

CHAPTER 9

Naval engagements

Don't talk to me about naval tradition. It's nothing but rum, sodomy and the lash.
— Sir Winston Churchill

My father served in the Australian Navy and so I was naturally well disposed towards the naval visits that our diplomats abroad are often called upon to facilitate. I hosted a number of them when I was in Ghana, Indonesia, and the Philippines where I had the opportunity to travel from Manila Bay to Subic Bay on the aircraft carrier HMAS Melbourne. The trip included a landing on the flight deck which looked decidedly small from the air compared with a normal landing strip, and even more nerve-wracking, transferring to another ship by a line suspended over the sea. It was rather scary as I could see several large sharks in the waters below.

But three visits in particular left a lasting impression.

The submarine HMAS Otway visited Tema, the port of Accra, on its way from England to Australia. A report of its arrival in the *Ghana Times* prompted an unsolicited visit from the paramount chief of Kibi, Nana Ofori Atta II. When he read that this vessel could travel under water he was intrigued and amazed, and donned his colourful robes of office and gathered several of his linguists (advisors) and set off in two Austin Princess cars from Kibi to Tema.

I explained to the captain of the Otway that his visitor was an important traditional chief from central Ghana with his retinue, and that they were curious to see the vessel for themselves. The group arrived in their dazzling robes beside the Otway in the late afternoon and the captain rose to the occasion. He assured them that the submarine could indeed submerge and travel under water, but also explained that unfortunately he could not dive the submarine for them in the harbour. He invited them to the officer's wardroom for refreshments where the chief and his retinue settled in for some serious drinking while officers took turns to host their colourful and curious visitors. They were still on board at 10 a.m. the next morning and the wardroom's stock of whisky, brandy, and cognac were seriously depleted, a loss I felt obliged to make up for from the High Commission's stocks.

The visit was a great success and enormous fun from beginning to end. When I had farewelled the captain and his crew and had been ceremonially piped ashore, a taxi screeched to a halt on the wharf. A large man with a bushy red beard, wearing only his underpants and one thong, leapt out and ran towards the Otway with the unpaid taxi driver in hot pursuit. Clearly he had no pockets and no wallet. It transpired that he was the Otway's cook. The taxi driver told me that he had been hired the day before and had visited various establishments, including as far afield as Kumasi in central Ghana. The captain said that experience suggested the irate taxi driver was probably telling the truth and asked me to pay him. The amount would be deducted from the cook's pay and transferred to me from the Otway's next port of call, Cape Town. I was told the cook was not allowed shore leave during that visit.

The second naval visit, which I have never forgotten, was the goodwill visit early in 1980 of the HMAS Derwent to Subic Bay. Two sailors on shore leave from the Derwent went into the Crocodile Bar in Olongapo City, famous for the two metre crocodile it kept in a pond near the bar and which the barman fed live chickens several times during the evening.

Our two noble sailors, emboldend by alcohol, took exception to this unusual show and remonstrated with the barman. He was unrepentant, and in the ensuing fight the barman's jaw was broken and the large mirror behind the bar smashed. Having disposed of the barman, our naval warriors now decided to release the unfortunate reptile. Wading into the pond, one locked his arms around the beast's jaws while the other grabbed its tail. They staggered out into the street with the writhing crocodile where, lacking the experience of the late Steve Irwin, they either lost their grip, their courage, or both, and tossed the creature away. Murphy's Law, that everything that could go wrong would go wrong, came into play with full force, or should I say full farce.

Unfortunately, the crocodile landed in the back of a passing jeepney, a decorated open form of public transport in the Philippines. Horrified passengers leapt out, one unfortunately being run over by another passing jeepney. Coming face to face with the enraged crocodile, the driver lost control of his vehicle, dislodged a column at the entrance of a neighbouring bar, crashed through the plate glass window, and injured some of its astonished patrons.

The crocodile, unharmed until now, ran into the street where it was, regrettably, run over by a passing truck. By now the street was in chaos. Despite their intake of alcohol, the intrepid sailors were aware that a crisis of considerable proportions was engulfing them tried to flee hotly pursued by the enraged bar owner, patrons, and a posse of police who finally caught them.

A substantial compensation claim arrived at the Australian embassy soon afterwards. Negotiations between officers of HMAS Derwent and numerous Filipino claimants resulted in the Derwent offering to pay damage claims that, including the structural damage to the bars, reached the impressive figure of $96,000. Embassy diplomats were able to reduce the claim to $50,000. The crew of the Derwent were so moved by the heroic, if costly attempt by their two fellow sailors to release the reptile — now deceased and part of the claim — and not wanting it to become an issue at Naval Headquarters in Australia, they raised the money to pay for the damages.

Despite the best endeavors of the embassy in Manila and of the Derwent to keep the incident quiet, the tale of the rescued crocodile quickly gained legendary status in the Philippines. Inevitably, a report under the headline 'Sailors' $50,000 Day Out at the Crocodile Bar' appeared on the front page of the *Sydney Morning Herald* in May 1980.

The third incident involved the HMAS Duchess's visit to Apia, Western Samoa, in 1973 for a meeting of the South Pacific Forum. The Duchess was supposedly there to provide communications between Apia and Canberra during the forum, although some cynics suggested that this was an Australian show of force reminiscent of nineteenth-century gunboat diplomacy.

The presence of the Duchess produced two amusing

incidents. Michael Somare, then prime minister of Papua New Guinea, was at Aggie Grey's Hotel dressed in a traditional lap-lap. A number of Australian sailors were also drinking there and, as he passed a table, one of them mistook him for a waiter said, 'Hey, bring us six more beers.' Unfazed, Michael returned a few minutes later with six beers on a tray. Smiling, he said, 'These are with my compliments.'

Later our prime minister, Gough Whitlam, appeared at the hotel and started chatting to a group of Australian sailors that included the cook from the Duchess. The cook, a corpulent, red-bearded man with a beer in hand said to Gough, 'Jeez, I'm glad to meet you. We are entertaining you in the wardroom on board tomorrow night. I'm preparing a special dinner menu for the occasion.' Gough replied, 'Good, what's on the menu?' The cook, having imbibed several beers replied, 'Mate, it's special for you. I'm preparing Chicken Whitlam. It's like your party. It's made up of left wings and bums.' Gough roared with laughter, but we understood the captain had to be dissuaded from punishing the cook for his *lese-majesty*.

Chicken Whitlam is served.

CHAPTER 10

Lost in translation

Translations (like wives) are seldom strictly faithful if they are in the least attractive. — Roy Campbell

I have always admired linguists, especially those with the ability to translate the nuances of one language into another, and have often regretted I was not one myself. While I spoke passable Russian and some Indonesian, both of which were of great value on my postings in the Soviet Union and Indonesia, I learned them rather like I learned algebra at school, that is with considerable effort.

I arrived in Leningrad (now St Petersburg again) fresh from a Russian language course at London University with my wife. During breakfast at the Astoria Hotel we observed at the neighbouring table a tall Englishman arguing in

English with a slow-witted Russian waiter. He was trying to order eight eggs, each boiled for three minutes, for himself and his wife and their two children. 'Don't you understand,' he roared, 'I want eight boiled eggs, two for each of us, all boiled for three minutes.'

I offered my assistance and said I was on my way to the Australian embassy in Moscow. I offered to tell the Russian waiter in Russian what he was trying to order. He glared at me and replied, 'I am Captain Talbot, the British Naval attaché. I speak fluent Russian, but the only way to get any service in this damned place is to shout at these peasants in English.' Put in my place, I retreated to observe some time later the arrival of three eggs which had apparently been boiled for eight minutes.

When the former trade minister and leader of the Country Party (now the National Party), 'Black Jack' McEwan, visited the General Assembly in New York he met Andre Gromyko, the Soviet foreign minister. Gromyko's intrepreter had trouble translating 'Country Party' and said, in Russian, the equivalent of, 'Minister, this is Mr John McEwan, the Leader of the Australian Peasants' Party.' Gromyko, who spoke good English himself, commented wryly, 'Peasants' Party? I didn't think Australia had one.'

I made my first visit to Palembang in southern Sumatra shortly after arriving in Indonesia. I still remembered some Malay and was learning Bahasa Indonesia, but I did not feel

Black Jack McEwan, leader of the 'Australian Peasants Party'.

confident enough to speak it in public. I decided to accept the embassy first secretary's offer to act as my interpreter. What ensued became a catalyst for my accelerated study of Indonesian.

'Ladies and gentlemen', I began, 'on behalf of my wife and myself, I want to say how delighted we are to be in Palembang.' The first secretary said a few words and, to my surprise, some men in the audience laughed, while some of the ladies blushed. By saying in Indonesian, *di atas istri saya,* and omitting the word *nama* before *istri,* he had in fact translated my opening as, 'Ladies and gentlemen, on top of my wife, I am delighted to be in Palembang'.

I chose the wrong location in which to make my first speech in Indonesian. It was in Mataram, the capital of the island of Lombok, a province with its own distinct dialect. After I had uttered a few sentences, the wife of the governor turned to my wife and asked in impeccable English, 'What language is your husband speaking?'

When I was leaving Indonesia to be ambassador to the Philippines, the former Indonesian foreign minister and vice president, Adam Malik, held a farewell reception for my wife and I. Malik had a kind heart, but a less generous command of English. In his farewell remarks, he said of my departure for Manila, 'Indonesia's gain will be the Philippines' loss.' An aide whispered in his ear that it should have been the other way around. A Russian linguist in

Moscow once said to me, 'They say that in capitalist countries man exploits man, but here, in the Soviet Union, it is the other way around.'

Australian slang often troubles the best interpreters. On a prime ministerial visit to Japan, Bob Hawke addressed a breakfast for members of the Japanese diet (parliament), most of whom spoke little or no English. His theme was his government's success in reducing strikes on the waterfront so that Australia could now be regarded with confidence by Japanese importers as a reliable supplier.

During the question period that followed a member of the diet asked Hawke if he could say something about the effect of union strikes on Australian exports to Japan. Hawke was irritated as this matter had been fully covered in his speech and said, 'I have just been talking about that. As I said, it isn't a problem now. I am not here to play funny buggers with you.'

For the Japanese interpreters, however, this was a real problem. They went into a huddle to consult on the best way to render Hawke's phrase 'funny buggers' into Japanese. After consultations, the chief interpreter said something in Japanese and the diet members looked bewildered and muttered to each other. I asked the interpreter nearest to me how this phrase had been translated. She replied, 'We really did not know what Mr Hawke meant. We discussed several possibilities. The chief interpreter used words which when translated back into English mean, 'I am not here to play laughing homosexuals with you.'

Foreign minister Bill Hayden once suggested to Prince Ranariddh of Cambodia at a meeting in New York about the political future of his country, that it seemed that the problem lay with the leaders of the various political factions, including the prince himself, who all wanted to be the *head sharang*. This was too much for the prince's embarrassed interpreter who spoke elegant French and good English, but was understandably unfamiliar with the Celtic words in the Australian slanguage. Our side also had its problems because we could not let our eyes meet in case we could no longer suppress our laughter. My deputy was finally able to control himself to offer the phrases *leading contender* and *top dog*. The prince at least understood the first phrase.

Similarly, our trade minister, Michael Duffy, once told a group of South American senior officials that the position they were adopting on free trade in agriculture was likely to be overtaken at the next meeting. Duffy, a horseracing enthusiast, bewildered the Spanish interpreter by saying, 'Many a favourite is run down in the last furlong of the race.'

On an occasion in West Africa, my wife was hosting a ladies tea party. We had ordered a load of manure for the garden two days previously. Without forewarning, a horse and dray heaped with manure came up the drive while the tea party was under way. The head houseboy, an inimitable character from the north of Ghana, entered and announced in a loud voice, 'Madam, the shit has arrived.' In a slightly admonishing tone, my wife said, 'Thank you, but in English we call that manure.' He replied, 'Maybe madam, but in our language we call it shit.'

Mistranslations from French offer a mine of humour. Despite his command of French leaving something to be desired, one of our senior ambassadors had been posted to France. In one of his speeches he looked back over his career and divided it into two, unfavourably comparing his rather dull postings before Paris with the cultural richness of the life he enjoyed in Paris. What he actually said in French, which greatly amused his audience, was '*quand je regarde derriere* ...', which means, 'when I look at my backside, I find it is divided into two parts'.

French is also a language that has seriously challenged the linguistic talents of President Bush. When discussing the decline in the French economy with the British prime minister, Tony Blair, in 2003 he famously said in a bizarre linguistic twist, 'The problem with the French is that they don't have a word for *entrepreneur*.'

One of the many unforgettable characters I met in my diplomatic career was the French ambassador to the UN during the 1980s. His grandfather had been a Georgian cavalry officer who had fled to France after the Russian revolution, and he was blessed with an excellent sense of humour and a good command of English, if heavily accented.

When I had dinner with him shortly before he was to visit Australia I asked him what airline he was flying. 'Kuntarse,' he replied. I almost choked on my aubergine before explaining to him the misunderstandings that could arise from his pronunciation. After roaring with laughter we had several minutes of pronunciation practice; *Q-ant-ass*, *Q-ant-ass*, he kept repeating. Also in Paris, when an Australian TV presenter was interviewing the wife of the late president François Mitterand, she asked what Madame Mitterand wanted most in her life. 'Apenis,' she replied. 'Yes,' the smart interviewer said, 'we all seek happiness'.

English to Chinese translation is often fraught with difficulty and filled with the potential for error. When Kevin Rudd was second secretary at our embassy in Beijing in 1984, his translation of ambassador Ross Garnaut's remarks to a Chinese delegation was greeted with laughter. Garnaut's comment that Australia and China were enjoying a great closeness in their relationship was rendered in Rudd's then imperfect Mandarin as, 'Australia and China are enjoying simultaneous orgasms in their relationship.' Kevin later became fluent in Mandarin before leaving the foreign service to enter politics.

I sought a meeting in early 2007 with the former personable and highly effective Chinese ambassador, Fu Ying. Her secretary asked me in English, 'Do you want to meet her on the telephone, or would you like to meet her face on face?' While reluctant to correct her English, I replied that I would indeed like to meet her face *to* face.

I avoid singing in public for reasons that, to anyone who has heard me, would be obvious. However, on a visit to Tokyo I found myself in a karaoke establishment with a fluent Japanese-speaking colleague who, because of his opposition to our participation in the Vietnam War, had resigned from the department to take up a professorship in Japan.

After a few too many sakes we were persuaded to mount the stage and sing an Australian song. We were stuck to know what to sing; 'Waltzing Matilda' seemed a little obvious, and we didn't know enough of the words of 'Wild Colonial Boy'. We had both been at the Royal Australian Air Force language school at Point Cook near Melbourne and had once sang a bawdy undergraduate duet on a dining-in night. Devoid of other ideas, and confident that no one in this audience would understand the words, we launched into a robust rendition of 'A Soldier Told Me' to the tune of the well-known Anglican hymn, 'Oh God, our help in ages past'.

> A soldier told me before he died,
> However hard he tried and tried,
> His wife was never satisfied.
> So he fashioned an organ of tempered steel,

Driven by a pulley and a bloody great wheel.

We roared. The audience was very responsive and we continued with elaborate gestures:

Round and round went the bloody great wheel,
In and out went the tool of steel
Until at last, his wife she cried,
Enough, enough I'm satisfied.
But this was a case of the biter bit,
There was no way of stopping it …

Prudence constrains me from recounting the tragic ending to this ballad. By now the crowd was applauding and cheering. Amazingly, an encore was called for and so we sang the same song again.

As we walked from the stage we were virtually mobbed, and I was even asked for an autograph. Feeling rather elated we returned to the bar where a well-dressed Japanese man stopped us and said in unusually good English, 'Congratulations, that was marvellous — hardly diplomatic, but a great presentation. Actually, I haven't heard it since I was at a party at the Australian National University where I taught Japanese for several years.' Undiplomatic certainly, and despite its popular reception we hoped that he was the only person in the audience who understood the words.

As Vietnam was moving towards a market economy in the 1990s the government wanted to develop both domestic and foreign capital markets. Seeking to attract foreign capital the Bank of Vietnam wanted a slogan in English and engaged a local advertising firm. The Vietnamese currency unit is the *dong* which unknown to the locals is one of many words in Australian slang used to describe the male organ. The slogan was duly launched in Hanoi and Ho Chi Minh City with considerable fanfare. It proclaimed, 'Invest in Vietnam. Your dong will be safe in our hands'. Sadly, the slogan was withdrawn when a visiting Australian banker pointed out the double meaning.

My wife and I, together with the British ambassador and his wife made a visit to the small northern Philippine island-province of Camiguin. The governor welcomed us at an arrival ceremony in the Tagalog language. The people of the Philippines are renowned for their warmth and friendliness, but we suspected that the governor's welcoming words were somewhat lost in translation when his interpreter said in English, 'Welcome to paradise. Our people greet you with open arms, open hearts, and open legs.'

One of the most effective interpretations — a non-interpretation actually — that I have encountered was when an Asian foreign minister was addressing a banquet in Seoul. He opened his speech in English with a rather long and complex joke. The Korean interpreter was lost, but did not show it. He uttered a few sentences and the audience laughed and applauded. The minister was impressed, and after the speech congratulated the interpreter for being able to condense his opening joke and still convey its meaning. The interpreter replied, 'Frankly, minister, I did not understand your joke so I said in Korean that the minister has now told his obligatory introductory joke, would you all please laugh heartily and applaud.'

Diplomats, especially those in the international bureaucracy, have developed a subtle language known as double-speak for concealing the true meaning of what they are saying. Here are some examples:

The valuable statement	*We agree with it*
The statement	*We disagree with it*
I have perused the documents	*I have not actually read the documents*
I have thoroughly read the documents	*I was fortunate enough to find a misprint in paragraph 498 which I will now point out*
While we agree in principle	*We disagree in practice*
We have a position of principle on this matter	*We have been consistently bloody-minded*

Lost in translation

The comprehensive and detailed statement	*The statement is too bloody* *long*
The distinguished and well informed representative	*One of ours*
The representative	*One of theirs*
And in conclusion	*I think I am somewhere* *near the end of my speech*
And finally	*I think I am somewhere* *near the end of my speech*

CHAPTER 11

A straight flush & foreign affaires

The zest goes out of a beautiful waltz when you dance it bust to bust. — Joyce Grenfell

The Department of Foreign Affairs and Trade has not sought to intrude into the sexual preferences of officers, male or female, provided their activities do not result in scandal or criminal activities. At a round of promotions several years ago there were ten candidates, five heterosexuals and five homosexuals for five assistant secretary positions. When the five gay people were all promoted and none of the heterosexuals, a disgruntled poker-playing heterosexual described the process as a 'straight flush'.

One male officer, after working in John Howard's office went on to become our ambassador to Sweden and then to the Netherlands, raised some eyebrows when he took his male partner on his first formal call on the Dutch queen. A Sydney tabloid reported the visit under the headline, 'Three queens at the palace'. Another male officer, an ambassador to the UN, had a West African partner, known at the mission as 'black rod' (an allusion to a position in the Australian senate), living in the residence. The issue can be tricky as many countries have less liberal attitudes than Australia. But the department can hardly be accused of anti-gay prejudice.

When I was ambassador to the Philippines the columnist Phillip Adams, then with the *Age*, accused the embassy of following a 'butch Australia' policy when a gay friend of a friend of his was denied a visa. It prompted the following exchange between us.

Dear Richard

You may recall from our halcyon days on the Australia Council that a number of Australia's leading writer, poets and painters were homosexual. Astonishingly this also applied to some of our ballet dancers, and I am led to believe that this particular sexual deviation is not entirely unknown in foreign affairs. Given Australia's woldwide reputation for sophistication in such matters, it is not surprising that congress between adult deviates is no longer an offence in the ACT. So I was surprised to learn that your people in Manila are applying a butch Australia policy in lieu of the 'white Australia' policy, that is they are refusing tourist visas on the grounds that they are poofters.

A dear old friend of mine, Mr Paul Blitz, is currently in Manila trying to arrange a visa for his friend, one Cezar ... As I understand it ... is in his late twenties and has visited Australia as a tourist for a period of six months. After returning to Manila and waiting the usual period, he applied for a new visa. Representations began in August last year and were all mysteriously rejected. Finally Blitz spoke to a Mr ... who made it clear that Cezar is to be denied his visit from Bosie (sic).

The grounds for the refusal were explicit. He has already had a trip to Australia and return trips for poofters are frowned upon. Having narrowly survived Nazism it is sad to see him suffering at the hands of ocker philistinism. I know him to be an honourable man who has dealt candidly with the matter. He would not attempt to embarrass Immigration by trying to keep him in Australia. I would appreciate your views on this matter or, better still, your personal intervention.

Regards,
Phillip Adams

A butch Australia policy?

Dear Phillip

I have received your 'blitz' on our alleged butch Australia policy and am personally reviewing the case. As a former colleague on the Arts Council, a member of a naval family, and a former inmate of a monastic boarding school some forty miles from Melbourne, I am, while not a member of gay liberation myself, aware of the growth of homosexuality and of the increasing tolerance of this practice.

Your telegram does, however, pose a problem for me, and like the monarch who found himself shipwrecked with his court jester on a desert island, I am at my wit's end. And like the lady who found on her wedding night she had unknowingly married a homosexual, I do not know which way to turn.

Like many public servants confronted with a complex situation and with their initiatives somewhat rusty from disuse, I have turned to Canberra for advice on this case. I am awaiting a reply. Meanwhile, please rest assured there were reasons for the earlier refusal of the visitors visa to Blitz which are not related to the homosexual apsect. I shall write again later.

Regards,

Dick

On an official flight in our sturdy DC-3, I had given a lift to a well-known Australian architect at that time resident in Jakarta. We flew across West Kalimantan over the mighty

Kapuas River and stopped overnight at a guesthouse in Pontianak. We had to share rooms. Naturally, I shared with my wife. A worried third secretary who was sharing a room with the architect, a strongly built tennis partner of mine, came to me and said, 'Please, I must change rooms. I watched him unpack a sarong and his hairdryer and I think he must be gay.' I admitted that he had a good mane of hair but that he also had a statuesque wife and two children and I assured him he would be quite safe. There was no 'butch Australia' policy at our embassies in Manila or Jakarta, or on our official tours.

An amusing heterosexual incident also occurred while I was in the Philippines. Our senior immigration officer was concerned about the number of elderly Australian males who sought visas to take newly acquired young Filipino brides to Australia. Confronted by an elderly man in his early eighties seeking a visa for his 20-year-old bride to be, he decided to offer some friendly advice, 'Have you considered, that given the age difference, attempts to consummate the marriage could result in death.' The grizzled former World War II digger reflected for a moment and then replied, 'No, not really. But if she dies, she dies.'

During our training course, we were told that tact had been identified by Sir Ernest Satow as one of the most vital characteristics of a diplomat. Our lecturer elaborated with an example that, although said in jest, has remained in my mind. The purser of a ship was instructing a young candidate for a cabin steward's position:

> I shall give you a practical example of tact. One morning on my rounds I entered a cabin believing it to be empty. Hearing running water and thinking a tap had been left on I entered the bathroom only to be confronted by a lady under the shower. I said I beg your pardon, Sir. Well, she thought that I thought she was a man and was less embarrassed by my intrusion. That, my boy, is tact.

Several days later the purser encountered the steward holding his head and with a bleeding nose outside of a cabin. The purser demanded to know what had happened.

> On previous mornings I have brought the tea into the cabin, the man has been in the top bunk and the lady in the bottom bunk. This morning they were both in the bottom bunk. Recalling your advice on tact I said: 'Do you two gentlemen both take milk and sugar with your tea?'

In diplomatic life, it is a pleasure to travel with one's children, but it can have its complications and give rise to situations calling for negotiations. On one occasion, we visited a rather large and overweight African chief. He had a retinue of young men and was obviously taken by our blonde second son. While the high commissioner (me) and his wife received only smiles, limp handshakes, and warm drinks he presented my son with what appeared to be a large and heavy gold ring. A few days later it fell on a tiled floor, breaking apart and revealing it was actually made of lead covered by a fine coating of gold.

On another chiefly visit near the border between Ghana and Burkino Faso — previously called Upper Volta, but renamed after a coup in the local language as the *land of incorruptible men* — it was my daughter's turn to attract attention. The local chief admired her blonde shoulder-length hair that he said looked like the tail of a white horse. He asked if he could have several strands, and then, taking me aside, lowered his voice and offered me two goats, two sheep, and five bush turkeys if we could lend her to his court until my next visit. Our daughter was hardly flattered by the offer. But diplomacy prevailed and we parted as friends when she agreed to surrender several strands of hair for which the chief insisted on giving me a bush turkey!

In Hanoi, we established a small mission shortly after the Vietnam war ended. Prime minister Whitlam was somewhat surprised when, on his first official visit, our gay charge d'affaires, recounting the difficulties of life in Hanoi, including finding suitable accommodation added in a pained voice, 'Both my handbags have been eaten by rats in my bedroom.'

At one of our posts, a senior and somewhat status-conscious ambassador had an eligible daughter spending a year with him. He hoped she might marry a young and suitable diplomatic colleague. Unfortunately, both his male third and first secretaries were recently married. Cunningly, he suggested to Canberra that for administrative and cost-cutting reasons — the latter always command attention at headquarters — the third secretary be replaced by a single male officer. The ambassador was, however, unpleasantly surprised when the newly arrived third secretary turned out to be very obviously gay and soon began a same-sex relationship with a local poet. Meanwhile, the ambassador's bored daughter finally found a boyfriend and, to the dismay and chagrin of her diplomatic father, eloped with a stable hand from her riding school. Ah, the best laid plans of mice and men — and diplomats — can come to grief.

While diplomats hardly rank with well-known political figures, actors, and sports stars in the gossip magazines and tabloid press, their indiscretions and peccadillos do not always pass unnoticed.

One of our ambassadors — on leave, of course — was standing outside a well-known brothel in Taipei, impeccably dressed except for his bare feet, when he encountered a member of our local mission's staff. Putting aside any embarrassment the ambassador, who was known to be tight-fisted over money, asked how he might recover his shoes and socks. The worldly staff member said, 'Oh, it is an established practice in these places. The ladies take your shoes, or sometimes even your trousers [as a certain prime minister was to discover] unless they are adequately recompensed for their services.' The shoes and socks were duly recovered after a top-up payment.

Another senior diplomat at the UN was surprised with his mistress by the unexpected return of his wife from a trip. Startled by her voice, he bundled his friend into the wardrobe, locked the door, and started to dress as quickly as he could. When his wife appeared he said he had not expected her so soon and that he was running late and changing for a committee meeting. He intended to release his mistress as soon as he could and smuggle her out of the apartment. But things went badly wrong when his wife found two female shoes — not her own — on the floor. Worse, hearing sounds coming from inside the wardrobe she opened the door and came face to face with the blushing interloper. After a heated exchange she saw the woman out, left her husband a terse note, and resumed the trip from which she had just returned early.

A more famous case involves the first prime minister of Malaysia, Tunku Abdul Rahman. He had studied law in

Diplomatic indiscretions do not always pass unnoticed.

England and had become a magistrate before entering politics. Prostitution was illegal in his court district at that time. One day a young woman was arraigned before him and, when asked to state her name, said with a sly smile, 'Don't be silly, you know very well who I am.'

'I know', said the magistrate, 'but its a legal requirement to confirm your identity'.

CHAPTER 12

Ministers and mandarins

Let us be grave. Here comes a fool.
—James Boswell, *Life of Johnson*

I have had the privilege of working closely or having some association with twelve foreign ministers and seven prime ministers, mostly before but also on two occasions after my retirement. Comparisons are odious and I do not intend to make them except to say that most were stimulating and intelligent, and welcomed frank advice on our foreign, security, and trade policy interests. Often they were entertaining to be with on a personal as well as an official basis. Sir Garfield Barwick and Andrew Peacock on the Liberal side, and Gough Whitlam, Bill Hayden and Gareth Evans on the Labor side fall into this category.

Predictably, however, there were a number of occasions when there were amusing or undiplomatic moments.

As the *New Yorker* suggested in a cartoon I have always remembered from the mid-1980s, some ministers of foreign affairs are prone to pomposity, arrogance, and the pursuit of personal publicity. It showed a group of dark-suited officials carrying briefcases about to call on the minister. The leading official was saying, 'The important thing one needs to know about the foreign minister is that, by and large, he is full of baloney.' Certainly, some foreign ministerial egos respond all too readily to the courtesies and ceremonial receptions in influential world capitals; others, like Tony Street (Liberal) and Don Willesee (ALP), were modest, unassuming, and not at all captivated by the trappings of office.

Gareth Evans put it neatly when he said he had been 'a little envious' of some favourable publicity I had received adding, 'I don't care how many prima donnas there are around here as long as I am *prima donna assaluta*!' Gareth and I worked out cooperative ground rules for the minister-mandarin relationship which we both believe were productive between 1988 and 1992.

Foreign minister Alexander Downer said of Opposition leader Kevin Rudd in April 2007 that 'he just loves publicity', adding that 'the more you love publicity, the more trouble you get into'. It was strange he chose to say this in a two-part ABC television *Australian Story* profile in which

'Prima donna assaluta.'

he had sought to participate against the advice of his senior staff.

The public probably thinks that the problems of diplomacy are only with foreign governments. The reality is that the most difficult governments and ministers, with which a diplomat has to deal, are often their own. A foreign minister's statements, unlike those of ministers in domestic portfolios, can result in positive or negative reactions in other parts of the world. This imposes an obligation on foreign ministers to show discretion and cultural sensitivity when making comments. As former British prime minister Harold McMillan once said, a foreign secretary is always in danger of 'being poised between a cliché and an indiscretion'. Some are eminent enough to disregard such concerns. When chided by a political colleague about not showing sufficient gratitude 'to those splendid Americans' when they entered World War II, Winston Churchill said, 'What do you expect me to do? Kiss the president on all four cheeks?'

Afficionados of the BBC's *Yes Minister* are well aware of the amusing manipulations and petty deceptions that can occur between ministers and their senior advisors. Former prime minister Malcolm Fraser and the then head of his department, Sir Geoffrey Yeend, once watched an episode together when Malcolm was in hospital. A nurse commented later, 'Oh, they both enjoyed it, but I noticed they laughed at different times.'

A classic example of the *Yes Minister* syndrome occurred when Paul Hasluck, then foreign minister, asked the secretary, Jim Plimsoll, to prepare a submission arguing that Radio Australia — which was causing the government a great deal of embarrassment because of its reporting on and broadcasts into Asia — should be removed from the Australian Broadcasting Commission and placed under the direct control of the Department of External Affairs.

I was at that time the department's first public information officer and strongly opposed to such a manoeuvre. I argued that Radio Australia would come to be seen simply as the voice of the government, like Radio Moscow, and South-East Asian listeners would look to other broadcasters for independent news. Plimsoll did not want a confrontation with Hasluck and put the minister's request and my notes for a reply in his commodious 'pending' tray.

After several weeks another note arrived from Hasluck's office asking for a prompt response to the minister's original request. Again Plimsoll did not respond. I was posted overseas but I gather such exchanges continued. Ultimately, Hasluck was appointed governor-general and the issue died. When I discussed the matter with Jim Plimsoll later, he replied in the best tradition of Sir Humphrey that you should always remember 'inactivity is a policy' you can often count on when all else fails.

As head of the amalgamated Department of Foreign Affairs and Trade I worked for two ministers, Gareth Evans and Michael Duffy. Serving two masters was not always easy. Once, when speaking to Duffy about a trade policy matter on the direct line to his office, Evans called on another direct line. When my secretary told him that I was speaking to the minister, Gareth, overlooking the fact that I served two ministers, replied tersely, 'What? I am the bloody minister.'

On another occasion, while attending a meeting of all of Canberra's heads of departments, Gareth called and was told that I was in a meeting. Ten minutes later he called again and told my secretary, 'Tell Dick I need to speak to him urgently. I would assume his minister takes precedence over a meeting of the local Sir Humphreys.'

Most of the prime ministers and foreign ministers with whom I have travelled or worked had a sense of humour. While Robert Menzies did not suffer fools gladly, nor did he succumb to pomposity. Unlike some of his successors, he was never seduced by the aura of the US presidency, and he once quipped that on his final call on President Eisenhower in his latter days in the White House, he came away feeling he had visited 'the tomb of the known soldier'.

On another occasion I was with him in a lift at the Savoy Hotel in London. The New Zealand prime minister, Sir Keith Holyoake, was also in the lift. Before alighting at his floor, Holyoake made a somewhat pompous comment about the British prime minister's chairmanship of the conference. As the doors closed, Menzies raised his bushy eyebrows and said in stage voice, 'Ah, great holy oaks from little acorns grow.'

De mortuis nil nisi bonum — speak no ill of the dead — is a well known maxim. But it would be remiss of me not to recall one of the major diplomatic fiascos in which I was involved. Dr H.C. 'Nugget' Coombs and I had drafted a speech for prime minister William McMahon to give at a White House dinner in October 1971. President Nixon spoke eloquently off the cuff. McMahon felt he should do likewise, and our draft never left his folder as he embarked on a rambling response which would have had Shakespeare groaning in his grave.

For his *pièce de résistance,* McMahon said, 'I take as my text a few well-chosen words. There comes a time in the life of a man in the flood of time that taken at the flood can lead on to fortune …' With the exception of the embarrassed Australians — one of whom reportedly groaned, 'I wish I was an Italian' — all the journalists listening to his words of wisdom in an adjacent room split their sides.

In an ironic epilogue a year later, Gough Whitlam, then prime minister, visited Washington and based his address to the National Press Club on an updated but basically identical original draft. This time there was no extempore

'There comes a time in the life of a man in the flood of time ...'

disservice to *Julius Caesar* and the speech was well received.

Ambassador Jeane Kirkpatrick, who died in December 2006, was a good friend and colleague at the United Nations. She was, however, a veteran cold war warrior and was not at all interested in disarmament. Foreign minister Bill Hayden, an advocate of disarmament and the banning of nuclear tests in all environments, had asked me to arrange a meeting with her. Because of their widely differing views, Jeane was reluctant, but I was eventually able to persuade her.

After Hayden arrived in New York he changed his mind about the meeting and it fell to me to cancel it. I telephoned Jeane and pleaded a 'diplomatic illness'. Unfortunately, later that day Bill and his wife were strolling down Park Avenue and as they passed the Waldorf Astoria, where Jeane was staying, they virtually bumped into each other. The next morning at the UN Jeane commented that Bill looked in excellent health. It's a tangled web a diplomat is sometimes called upon to weave, and all I could say was that he had made a surprisingly speedy recovery.

Bill Hayden had a sharp sense of humour. Once when asked at a press conference in New York about what transpired at an official meeting with the foreign minister of Mongolia, he reflected for a moment and said with a straight face, 'We enjoyed a yak together.'

One expects cartoonists to lampoon ministers, but one hardly expects TV news bulletins to do so, even inadvertently. During an SBS evening news bulletin in January 2006, while foreign minister Alexander Downer was speaking a box appeared at the top right corner of the screen with the words 'shows signs of brain activity'. This was presumably not a reference to Downer, but to a previous item about the health of the former prime minister of Israel, Ariel Sharon, who had suffered a severe stroke.

Of all my recollections of undiplomatic activities related to ministers — in this case a future prime minister — few can rival a visit to Indonesia in 1975 of the then president of the Australian Council of Trade Unions. But this is also a story of the triumph of the will and of redemption. Bob Hawke and Jim Ralston visited Jakarta to express the concern of the ACTU about Indonesian policy towards East Timor. The day they arrived in Jakarta I was hosting a black-tie diplomatic dinner to farewell the departing Austrian ambassador.

I told Bob and Jim that they were welcome to attend, but cautioned them that while they would get a good meal they might find it rather boring. Somewhat to my surprise they said they would like to come. The Austrian ambassador had requested a black tie dinner, but I offered to lend them long-sleeved batik shirts which they would find more comfortable, and which Indonesians regarded as formal. I said I would place several shirts on a bed in an upstairs bedroom for them.

Ralston was shorter and plumper than Hawke, and when they appeared they had obviously donned the wrong shirts — Ralston was wearing the large one, and Hawke the tight one. No matter, Indonesian beer and Australian wines flowed freely, and Hawke added zest to what would have been a routine diplomatic function.

Towards the end of the dinner the Austrian ambassador said, 'Mr Hawke, it has come to the ears of our ambassador in Canberra that you may have political ambitions beyond your union interests. May I ask you if that is true?' Hawke put down his tankard of beer, wiped some froth from his lips, looked the ambassador in the eye and replied, 'Ambassador, you are fuckin' well lookin' at the future prime minister of Orstralia.' I often wondered how the Austrian ambassador, a punctilious man not known for his informality, reported this important piece of accurate information to his foreign ministry in Vienna.

More spectacular events were to occur the following evening. It had been arranged for Hawke to call on Indonesia's foreign minister, Adam Malik, at his residence in Menteng at 6.00 p.m. I was to accompany our treasurer, Phillip Lynch, who was also in Jakarta, on a call on the minister for finance. So, I had arranged for an Indonesian speaking third secretary from the embassy to meet Hawke at the Hotel Indonesia. I would meet them at Malik's residence.

When I arrived I was received by Malik and four officers from the Indonesian foreign ministry, all were formally dressed in suits. There was no sign of Bob Hawke or our third secretary. Some twenty minutes later, however, dogs started barking and Hawke appeared through a side gate, entirely relaxed if a little unsteady on his feet. Our third secretary looked pale and under some stress. After the introductions and a perfunctory apology for his lateness, Malik welcomed Hawke saying, 'I hope you have had a useful day. I understand Agus Sudono [the president of the Indonesian trade union movement, SOBSI] has briefed you on our union activities.'

Hawke slapped his thigh and replied, 'Adam, we're old friends, let's cut out the bullshit. Your trade unions are worth four-fifths of five-eights of fuck all.' There was a pregnant pause before Hawke told the third secretary, 'Translate what I have said.'

'I can't, Mr Hawke,' he replied. Malik smiled and said helpfully, 'He doesn't need to.'

Changing the subject Hawke then asked, 'Adam, have you got a decent cigar? Surely Marcos must have given you a box on one of your visits to the Philippines.'

Malik replied, 'I have both Philippine and Cuban cigars upstairs. I will get you a couple.' When Malik had gone, Hawke, apparently forgetting the presence of the four English speaking Indonesian foreign ministry officials,

'You're lookin' at the future prime minister of Orstralia.'

turned to me and said, 'Funny bastard, Malik; used to be a bloody communist and now here he is working for Soeharto's reactionary outfit.'

The next morning, I telephoned Malik to seek his views on how the meeting had gone. He was relaxed and understanding; Bob Hawke was a friend. The third secretary, as he had been trained to do, produced an accurate record of the conversation with some of Hawke's more colourful phrases in quotation marks. In a long diplomatic career, this was only one of two records of conversation which I chose to destroy rather than file because of the possible uproar should they have leaked at that time.

As I noted, this story is also one of redemption and triumph of the will. What Hawke told the Austrian ambassador came to pass. He had the willpower to give up alcohol and became a popular and successful prime minister of Australia from 1982 until 1991.

Of all the foreign heads of government I have met none was more accessible, informal, and charming than Tunku Abdul Rahman of Malaysia. Once on a Sunday morning, when I was acting high commissioner in Kuala Lumpur, I received a cable from Canberra asking me to convey an urgent message from prime minister Menzies to the Tunku about the proposed formation of Malaysia. When I telephoned the Tunku's private secretary, the Tunku himself answered the phone himself and asked me to come over immediately.

The Tunku was not only accessible, he also had a sense of humour. At an Australia Day reception he told our high commissioner, Tom Critchley, that he was confused over the resignation of the British defence minister, John Profumo, whom he had met and liked. Tom explained that Profumo had compromised himself by sharing a mistress with the Soviet naval attaché in London and then lying about the affair in the House of Commons. The Tunku smiled and replied, 'If we applied such a strict approach to private lives here some very good men might have to be excluded from Cabinet.'

The Tunku used to tell an amusing tale about a welcoming party that lined the road while he was returning to his home state of Kedah. It was the government's policy then to encourage Malays to have large families and the Tunku stopped to talk to a Malay man and his wife surrounded by a dozen children. He shook the man's hand and asked if all the children were his. The Malay beamed and said, 'Yes, Tunku.'

'Congratulations,' he replied, 'you deserve a knighthood.'

At this point the Malay's wife smiled and observed, 'Tunku, he has a night-hood. The problem is he doesn't wear it!'

Contacts between ministers and mandarins often extend

Angling for the 'floating squash players' vote?

beyond their normal official contacts. Prime minister Billy McMahon loved squash. I was a foreign affairs advisor to Billy in 1971 and 1972 and accompanied him on most of his overseas trips and I suspect that one of my roles was to be his squash partner. Indeed, this was a more exacting task than advising him on foreign policy issues. Once, in London, he ran in front of me at the last moment and my raquet struck him on the nose, opening up a deep wound shortly before he was to appear on BBC television. I had a doctor patch up his nose as well as he could, but unfortunately Billy looked a bit like a parrot with a fractured beak during his TV interview.

About the same time, there were press reports in Australia that I might go into politics. My denials of any such intentions were, however, lost to a jocular quip that I was not trying to capture the 'floating squash players' vote'.

In November 1972 before the general election — which McMahon lost to Gough Whitlam — he telephoned to ask me to play squash with him in Canberra. I was chairing an interdepartmental meeting at the time, and had to decline. This resulted in his wife telephoning my wife and saying Billy was depressed, really needed a game and the exercise, and asked whether I could be persuaded. There was even an oblique reference to 'rats leaving the sinking ship'. Birgit called me. I said I simply could not cancel the meeting I was to chair, but I would arrange for Dennis Richardson, then a rising star in foreign affairs and our present ambassador in Washington, to play with McMahon.

Dennis agreed, collected his squash gear and was hurrying to the Manuka squash courts where he suddenly realised the only T-shirt in his kit was an ALP 'It's Time' election shirt. Discretion was the better part of valour. He hurried home to collect a different shirt and arrived ten minutes late for the game. He was chided for being late but Billy got the game he wanted. Such obligations — above and beyond the call of duty — are a less well-known aspect of the job.

The only minister with whom I have fallen out in the last forty years is Alexander Downer. This was due not to any clash of personality — indeed, I was happy to provide advice to Downer before and after the March 1996 election — but to disagreements about which policies would best serve Australia's interests, especially in relation to East Timor, Iraq, the Middle East, the United Nations, and an Australian republic.

Prime Minister John Howard and Foreign minister Downer have both had a tendency to make bombastic statements for domestic political advantage and to pursue policies with excessive zeal. For example, John Howard's assertion of the right to strike pre-emptively at neighbouring states thought to be harbouring terrorists. Such statements are counter-productive and have a

'Megaphone diplomacy.'

Embassy of the Islamic Republic of Iran
Manila

Rec 22/4

IN THE NAME OF GOD

Note No. 3380

The Embassy of the Islamic Republic of Iran has the honour to inform all the Diplomatic and Consular Missions and International Organizations in the Philippines of the following Islamic ideological principle and belief concerning shaking hands among Islamic men and women during a social gathering:

1. An Islamic man cannot shake hands with any woman, although he may shake hands with any man;
2. An Islamic woman cannot shake hands with any man, although she may shake hands with any woman.

The Embassy wishes to reiterate that the aforementioned Islamic custom which is being presently observed by the Islamic Republic of Iran is definitely not a sign of impoliteness but of great respect for any man or woman regardless of her or his creed or race.

Observance of the aforementioned is highly appreciated.

Wishing the victory of the oppressed over the oppressors.

June 14, 1982, Manila.

EMBASSY OF THE ISLAMIC REPUBLIC OF IRAN
سفارت جمهوری اسلامی ایران
مانیل
MANILA

All the Diplomatic & Consular Missions
And International Organizations
In the Philippines

damaging impact on foreign policy; they fall into the category of what Indonesian foreign minister Hassan Wirajuda has aptly called 'megaphone diplomacy'. Our ministers would be well advised to take Maurice de Talleyrand's advice to French diplomats, *n'ayez pas de zèle* — do not be overzealous.

In fact zealots and political ideologues make bad ministers and diplomats, and poor negotiators. Sound diplomacy requires a large measure of unemotional, apolitical, detached analysis and patience. I could quote many examples of undiplomatic, but not necessarily amusing statements designed to serve a political purpose, such as playing on fear of Islamic extremism during an election campaign, and comments that play to latent racism and religious intolerance.

Ministers need to accept the limitations that Australia, as a middle-power, faces in the international community. John Howard's criticism of American Democratic presidential contender Barack Obama's approach to Iraq in 2007 was certainly unwise and suggests a sense of self-importance somewhat at odds with reality. Downer has a sense of humour and describes criticism of himself as like 'rubber bullets off a Sherman tank'. In some cases, however, it might have been helpful to him and to the country to have taken some notice of the so-called rubber bullets.

I am reminded of two revealing historical episodes.

When told of Russian naval activity in the Pacific before the Russian revolution, a minister was quoted as saying, 'I warn the Tsar'. A British foreign secretary, taking it for granted that London was at the very centre of the world, responded to reports of damage to the undersea cables between England and France during a fierce storm in the Channel, by saying that, 'unfortunately the Continent has been isolated'. A failure to adopt a realistic perspective of a nation's place in world affairs can leave one sounding rather foolish.

CHAPTER 13

WAWA — West Africa wins again

I speak of Africa and golden joy.
— William Shakespeare

I spent six years on the vast continent of Africa. It was an enriching experience from which I learned much. Anyone who has lived in Africa must be deeply touched by its vastness, its brilliant colors, its contrasts, its beauty, and despite the daunting difficulties most of them face daily, the charm, warmth, and humour of its peoples. Foreigners, however, need to adjust to a different tempo and rhythm of life.

Western diplomacy often involves a series of finely timed appointments. Punctuality and marking time by the clock is a very western European and American concept. One of the most common frustrations in West Africa, where I spent three years, is that planned schedules are disrupted and appointments often fall through.

In many countries in Asia, Africa, and South America time is elastic. I once asked a bus driver in West Africa, 'What time does your bus leave?' He replied, quite reasonably, 'When it's full.' In Spanish, the word *manyana* reflects a relaxed attitude to time. In Indonesia, there is a well-known phrase, *jam karet*, which means in English 'rubber time'. In Russia, the concept of immediacy is not readily translated: *nemyedleno* actually means 'not slowly', while *cei chas* means 'within the hour'.

In West Africa, time can be even more elastic. Early in our posting to Ghana, my wife and I received an invitation to attend a ceremony in a town about 40 kilometres from Accra. The printed invitation requested guests 'to be seated by 11 a.m'. We duly arrived at the town square at 10.55 a.m. It was deserted. There was no sign of any activity and I assumed we might have come to the wrong place.

Our driver made an enquiry and assured us we were at the right place, adding that, 'nothing is likely to happen for a while yet'. At about 12.15 p.m., a truck arrived carrying stacks of chairs, presumably those on which guests were supposed to have been seated since 11.00 a.m. Other guests had also started to arrive and we were glad to sit. At about

1.30 p.m. the district chief arrived and the ceremonies began.

Perhaps the clearest example of the different attitude to time involved a prominent chief from the north of Ghana. His eyesight had been failing for some time and the American ambassador had arranged for a Swiss optical firm based in Accra to test his eyesight and obtain glasses for him. The chief arrived at the firm's office, which was situated inside a department store, having made the long trip from the north. After he was tested he was asked to return in eight days to collect his glasses, which would be supplied from Switzerland. When the optician and the department store were about to close the chief was still in the waiting room. Politely, he was told the establishment was closing and to return in eight days time. The chief left but returned the next morning when the doors opened. This scene was repeated for eight days, with the chief arriving in the morning and leaving in the evening. Questioned about this, he said he had come to get glasses, and as he had plenty of time he would return home when his glasses arrived.

A former high commissioner in Kenya regularly invited the then Kenyan foreign minister to dinner at the Australian official residence. He would accept, but not appear. On one occasion when the Australian foreign minister was visiting Nairobi, the high commissioner was determined to secure the presence of the Kenyan minister and telephoned him several times. Despite his positive responses, the minister did not show up. The irritated high commissioner telephoned him the next morning to say how embarrassed he had been by his failure to turn up. The minister explained, 'I'm sorry, I was coming to have dinner with you, but I wasn't hungry last night.'

It is incumbent on Australian heads of missions overseas to mark Anzac Day each year. I wrote to the minister of defense in Accra asking whether he could provide a bugler to play the Last Post at the Dawn Service, which I would be conducting. I was amused by his unexpected offer of 'two burglars'.

One of the great characters we encountered in West Africa

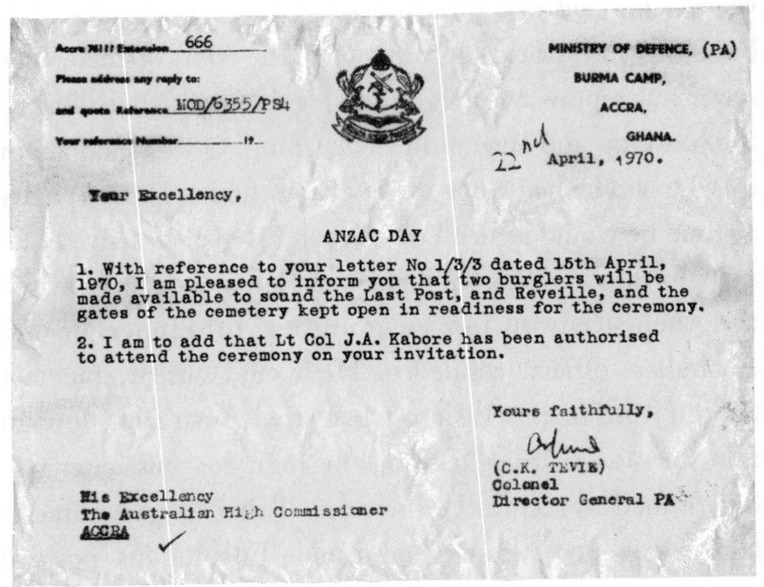

Accra 76111 Extension 666

Please address any reply to:

and quote Reference MOD/6355/PS4

Your reference Number ...... 19..

MINISTRY OF DEFENCE, (PA)
BURMA CAMP,
ACCRA,
GHANA.

22nd April, 1970.

Your Excellency,

ANZAC DAY

1. With reference to your letter No 1/3/3 dated 15th April, 1970, I am pleased to inform you that two burglers will be made available to sound the Last Post, and Reveille, and the gates of the cemetery kept open in readiness for the ceremony.

2. I am to add that Lt Col J.A. Kabore has been authorised to attend the ceremony on your invitation.

Yours faithfully,

(C.K. TEVIE)
Colonel
Director General PA

His Excellency
The Australian High Commissioner
ACCRA

was Tiyo, the chief of staff of the Australian official residence in Accra. He could be a rogue when it came to alcohol, especially whisky which he referred to as 'fire water' or the 'devil's drink', and we kept it locked up in the storeroom at all times. Once he hid a bottle of scotch during a reception and consumed most of it while trying to serve guests. My wife found him staggering around the bar with his red eyes rolling in all directions. Sensing what was coming, Tiyo protested, 'Madam, I swear by God I no touch drink.' Since he was not, as far as we knew, a believer this oath was hardly decisive. My daughter kept a pet squirrel in the residence and he imaginatively added, 'Maybe I been bitten by the squirrel.' But he was a gentle man with a heart of gold, a wonderful sense of humour, and was full of tales and wisdom.

During World War II, he had been recruited by the colonial power, Britain, to serve in a West African regiment and taken to Burma to fight the Japanese. After an unfortunate incident in which some Burmese were shot by members of the his regiment, Tiyo and several of his colleagues were addressed by a British officer who had with him two Burmese persons and two Japanese prisoners. He pointed to the Burmese and said, 'These be Burmese. They be good. You help them.' Turning to the Japanese, the officer said, 'These be Japan men. They be bad. You can shoot them.' At the end of the meeting, Tiyo imparted to the British officer an uncomfortable truth, saying, 'Thank you sir but there be big problem. To us Japan man and Burma man look the same.'

During the same campaign, Tiyo broke his big toe and found wearing his army boot painful. He told us how he took a stone and a long cord and climbed a nearby tree. He tied one end of the cord around his toe and the other end around the stone, steeled, himself and dropped the stone. He claimed this method of treatment, which he said was not uncommon in West Africa, straightened his broken toe and enabled him to wear his boot. Tiyo had the good fortune to escape a court martial and was instead returned to West Africa when, attempting to lighten the weight of his backpack, he threw a number of grenades into a river, one of which hit a rock and exploded, thereby risking exposing the position of his regiment to the Japanese.

On another occasion when we were hosting a dinner party, Tiyo entered unexpectedly, bowed, and announced in a grave voice, 'Hercules is dead.' This brought the conversation to a halt and we had to explain that Hercules was the master of a hutch of guinea pigs, belonging to our daughter, and that he had probably died from over-exertion or battling to maintain his status.

Sierra Leone was one of the countries in my area of responsibility in West Africa. On one visit we stayed at the City Hotel in Freetown in the room in which Graham Greene wrote some of his famous West African novel, *The*

Heart of the Matter. On the day of our departure, the resident British high commissioner and his wife offered to take us to the airport across the water in a former naval launch. We would see the waterways and the approach to the Freetown harbour and have a picnic lunch on the way. It seemed too good an opportunity to miss.

We dropped anchor in the bay near the mouth of the river. Under a tropical sun our host provided shade, beer, and gin and tonics. Nobody, including our driver — an elderly petty officer who the high commissioner's wife remarked had been somewhat vague since he was struck by lightning six months previously — noticed the tide was going out, and we soon found ourselves aground on a sandbank. Chicken sandwiches and more gin and tonics somewhat alleviated our concerns about catching our return flight while we waited for the tide to rise.

Finally, we had water under our keel and set off across the bay at full throttle towards the jetty near the airport. As we continued with our animated post-luncheon discussion of the situation in Sierra Leone we noticed a large black and red tanker coming in rapidly from the ocean to the port of Freetown. Given its size, we assumed our driver was aware of its presence. The ship was cutting through the water and bearing down on us at some speed and, as the gap narrowed, we nervously realised that our lightning-struck driver was determined to cut across its bow. Later, he would explain that he was trying to avoid the ship's large wake that would be uncomfortable for us in the launch.

My wife, alarmed that we were about to be rammed and sunk beneath the tanker's bow, cried out that if we had to jump overboard we should grab our passports, tickets, and currency and abandon the rest of our luggage. The high commissioner was apparently immobilised by a combination of heat and alcohol but, as the tanker's siren shrieked its warning, his wife — one of those strong, angular Anglo-Saxon women of the type who helped build the British empire — leapt into the cabin crying, 'You maniac, what the hell are you doing?' Throwing the petty officer aside, she seized the wheel and thrust the engine full throttle into reverse. We veered away from the tanker's hull — now towering above us — just in time, and found ourselves rolling and bobbing wildly in its wake. Even the comatose high commissioner was now alert. The collision averted and headlines about two diplomats and their spouses having perished at sea avoided, we continued on our way to the airport, and caught our flight, which was fortuitously running late.

As a footnote to this saga, one that luckily for us West Africa did not win, the British high commissioner later informed us that the petty officer had been made redundant and had received compensation for having been struck by lightning.

CHAPTER 14

Undiplomatic gifts

Beware the gift of a beast. — anon

Exchanges of gifts between governments have always been a part of diplomacy. But an inadequate attention to local cultural sensitivities can mean that things do not always run smoothly. An Australian prime minister once wanted to present the Agong (king) of Malaysia with some handcrafted Australian beer mugs. The Agong, as a devout Muslim, did not touch alcohol, and in any case Malaysia is well known for producing its own pewter mugs.

Prime minister Malcolm Fraser was persuaded to reject a proposal to present President Soeharto of Indonesia with a painting by the Australian artist Donald Friend who was living and painting in Bali at the time. Such a gift would have been a fine symbol of the example of the strong cultural association between Australia and Indonesia, but it was judged too sensitive because of Friend's homosexuality. A modern Australian abstract painting was presented instead, which was never hung in the palace or in the president's home and is now probably languishing in some Jakarta storeroom.

Searching for imaginative gifts for heads of government, Australian prime ministers have occasionally turned to that symbol of virility, the stud bull — with mixed results. When Gough Whitlam visited China on his first official visit he decided to present a stud bull to the Chinese government. The bull was flown to Beijing accompanied by its handler in advance of Whitlam's arrival. The strapping handler, with a reputation as a ladies' man in rural Victoria, was alleged to have unsuccessfully propositioned his room maid over several days at his hotel. When a senior official from Whitlam's party found himself sharing a lift at the hotel with the handler, he enquired after the bull. 'Poor bastard,' the handler replied, 'he was taken straight to one of the artificial insemination centres outside Beijing and put on the tube'. He paused reflectively, no doubt recalling his own unsuccessful efforts, and said philosophically, 'This is a strange place. It seems even a bull can't get a good root in China.'

'Comrade, think of it as the gift that keeps on giving.'

excreta tauri sapientiam fulceat

On his prime ministerial visit in 1976, Malcolm Fraser also thought that a Murray Grey bull would be an appropriate gift for former Indonesian president Soeharto, who had a farm at Tapos, near Bogor. My deputy at the embassy was blessed with a wry sense of humour, and on all cables to Canberra on this matter he placed the undiplomatic heading, 'Prime Ministerial Bull'. After several such cables we received a telephone call warning us that the prime minister was not amused. Being the respectful and dutiful public servants that we were, the heading was changed to 'Bull for President'. Regrettably, in retrospect, I did not accept the first alternative heading in Latin offered for the cable namely, *excreta tauri sapientiam fulceat* — which, according to my rusty Latin, means bullshit baffles brains.

The beast was flown on an RAAF C130 to Jakarta where the foreign minister, Adam Malik, was to receive it from me on behalf of the president before being trucked to Tapos. To ensure these somewhat risky arrangements proceeded smoothly, the handler had tranquilised the bull during the flight.

The C130 taxied towards the reception party and turned so its rear loading bay door could be lowered. It was one of those moments of eager anticipation. When the bay opened, what we saw was not a proud, snorting, red-blooded, symbol of Australian potency but a worried handler bending over a large, prone heap of bovine flesh. 'Oh God,' said one of my aides, 'it's dead!' The handler's attempt to arouse the beast must have been excessive for, with a roar, it suddenly rose to its feet, stumbled down the ramp and charged towards the alarmed party which scattered in all directions. Fortunately the handler, with the help of several Indonesian soldiers, was able to regain control of the bull and the handover from the relieved ambassador to a nervous foreign minister proceeded.

Regrettably, neither of these gifts — well-intentioned though they may have been — managed to perform their intended function in their new environments.

I travelled to Cambodia on a state visit with Harold Holt in 1967. In those days the prime minister used an RAAF Vickers Viscount aircraft for official travel of this nature. It was, of course, much smaller than the aircraft now used by the prime minister. Holt had given Prince Sihanouk a modest gift at the state dinner the evening before his departure and he was a little surprised that, apart from fulsome rhetoric, there was no gift in return. His surprise was, however, short-lived. At the ceremonial departure the following morning, a local band played a rousing version of 'Waltzing Matilda' — apparently unaware that it was not our national anthem — when a truck pulled up in front of the red carpet leading to our aircraft and lowered a large, elegantly carved stone elephant to the ground.

Prince Sihanouk had instructed the gift to be delivered to the plane just before Holt's departure. Thoughtfully, he had even sent six powerfully built Cambodian workers to load the elephant onto the Viscount. Our responsible RAAF captain paled at the sight of the elephant and said that, beautiful as it was, it simply could not be carried on the aircraft that was to fly on to Laos and then to Taiwan before returning to Australia. To decline the prince's gift would certainly detract from a successful visit and perhaps even cause a diplomatic incident. Honour was satisfied when the gift was showered with appreciation and the aerodynamic situation explained. It was agreed that it be sent by land and sea to find a resting place in the garden at the prime minister's Lodge in Canberra. Where it is now, I do not know.

On another occasion, a visiting Indonesian minister presented former foreign minister Paul Hasluck with a large stuffed Sumatran tiger. It was a magnificent creature, but conservationists and others thought that accepting it would send a poor message to the world. Hasluck overcame the problem by accepting the gift but passing it on to the Claremont Australian Rules Club in Perth, of which he was a supporter and which had a tiger as its logo.

As a footnote, my Australian embassy colleagues presented me with an undiplomatic gift when I completed my posting in Jakarta. I had been Australian ambassador there when Indonesia invaded and incorporated the former Portuguese colony of East Timor, and when prime minister Malcolm Fraser extended *de facto* recognition to the incorporation. They gave me a pewter beer mug on which the Melbourne *Age* masthead had been neatly etched and below it the headline:

FRASER RECOGNISES FRETELIN GOVERNMENT.
WOOLCOTT FIRST AUSSIE ENVOY.

CHAPTER 15

Undiplomatic cables

The phrase 'the attitude of France' should be used instead of the more ambiguous 'French position'.
— official cable to Canberra, 1979

These days, because diplomats are increasingly wary that their views may be used against them at some future time, they are more likely to communicate using email and telephone and leave no permanent record. Unfortunately, as a result, the amusing exchanges of cables — which officers often used to collect — are a thing of the past.

In a cable to Canberra on a likely cabinet reshuffle, our ambassador in Saigon noted sagely that, 'In my opinion Dung will be dropped at tomorrow's meeting.' Presumably he was referring to the former politician Tran Van Dung.

The following cables involve an exchange between foreign minister Gareth Evans, the late Dr Peter Wilenski, our ambassador to the UN, and myself in 1990 regarding our efforts to gain election to the Commission on Human Rights.

Our mission to the United Nation once suggested, perhaps unwisely, to foreign minister Bill Hayden, that he

RESTRICTED
FIRST

INFO: SEC
COPY NO. 1

INWARD CABLEGRAM

O.UN049686 ASCL
TOR 06.23 24.05.90

O.UN049686 1613 23.05.90 CLA FIRST

TO.
PP CANBERRA/7441

RP.
PP GENEVA/465 VIENNA/3124

FM. UN NEW YORK / FA

R E S T R I C T E D

CHR ELECTIONS: AUSTRALIA SCRAPES HOME

FROM AMBASSADOR

WE HAVE NON-STOP FOR THE PAST TEN DAYS TALKED, EATEN, DRUNK, CAJOLED, PERSUADED, LOBBIED, WINED, DINED, LUNCHED, ELBOWED, TRADED, STABBED, GOUGED, BREAKFASTED, COFFEED, ARGUED, PUSHED, PRESSURED, AND IN GENERAL HARMONIOUSLY COOPERATED WITH OUR DISTINGUISHED COLLEAGUES TO REVERSE OUR 1987 DEFEAT. THE RESULT WAS (WITH THE TOTAL VOTING BEING 54):

FIRST BALLOT PORTUGAL 41
FRG 41
AUSTRIA 41
AUSTRALIA 39
UK 39
(IRELAND 3)

SECOND BALLOT AUSTRALIA 31
UK 23

2. THANKS TO ALL WHO PARTICIPATED, INCLUDING THE WORK DONE OVER THE PAST SIX MONTHS IN GENEVA. FULL REPORT FOLLOWS.

ACTION: DEP FOREIGN + TRADE

MIN FOREIGN + TRADE MIN FOR TRADE NEGS

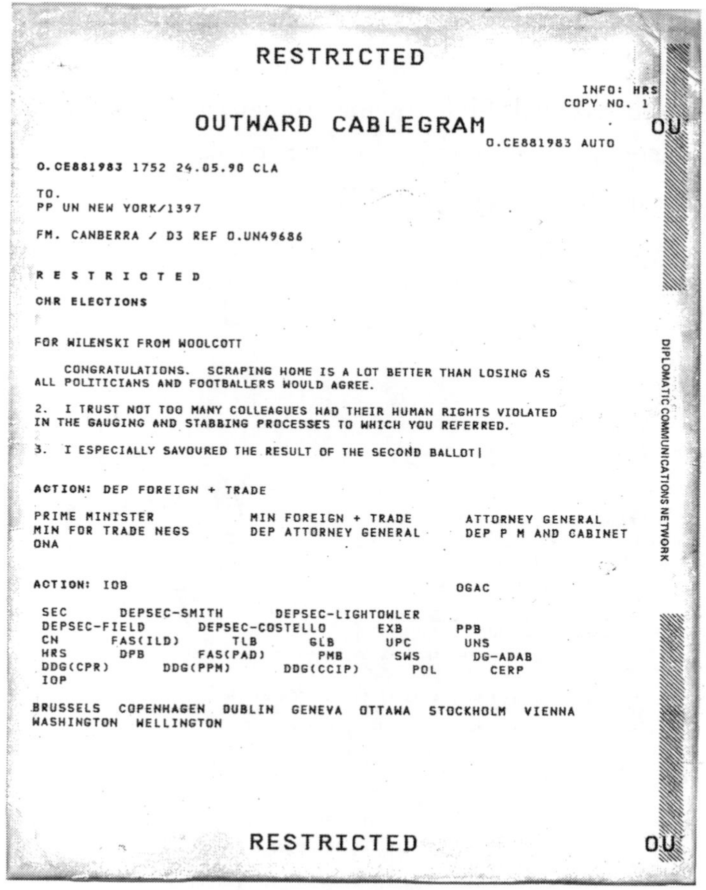

RESTRICTED

INFO: HRS
COPY NO. 1

OUTWARD CABLEGRAM

OU

O.CE881983 AUTO

O.CE881983 1752 24.05.90 CLA

TO.
PP UN NEW YORK/1397

FM. CANBERRA / D3 REF O.UN49686

R E S T R I C T E D

CHR ELECTIONS

FOR WILENSKI FROM WOOLCOTT

CONGRATULATIONS. SCRAPING HOME IS A LOT BETTER THAN LOSING AS ALL POLITICIANS AND FOOTBALLERS WOULD AGREE.

2. I TRUST NOT TOO MANY COLLEAGUES HAD THEIR HUMAN RIGHTS VIOLATED IN THE GAUGING AND STABBING PROCESSES TO WHICH YOU REFERRED.

3. I ESPECIALLY SAVOURED THE RESULT OF THE SECOND BALLOT!

ACTION: DEP FOREIGN + TRADE

PRIME MINISTER MIN FOREIGN + TRADE ATTORNEY GENERAL
MIN FOR TRADE NEGS DEP ATTORNEY GENERAL DEP P M AND CABINET
ONA

ACTION: IOB OGAC

SEC DEPSEC-SMITH DEPSEC-LIGHTOWLER
DEPSEC-FIELD DEPSEC-COSTELLO EXB PPB
CN FAS(ILD) TLB GLB UPC UNS
HRS DPB FAS(PAD) PMB SWS DG-ADAB
DDG(CPR) DDG(PPM) DDG(CCIP) POL CERP
IOP

BRUSSELS COPENHAGEN DUBLIN GENEVA OTTAWA STOCKHOLM VIENNA
WASHINGTON WELLINGTON

DIPLOMATIC COMMUNICATIONS NETWORK

RESTRICTED

OU

might discuss with the secretary general an issue relating to Cambodian representation during a lunch to which he had been invited. Hayden cabled in reply, 'How will I get our message to the secretary general at lunch — by semaphore?' Not to be outdone our mission replied, 'Worry not, Mission is hiring a bullhorn in case you find yourself sitting below the salt.'

I also received the following strange cable from the then minister of foreign affairs in Canberra about a curious report in the Sydney *Daily Mirror*.

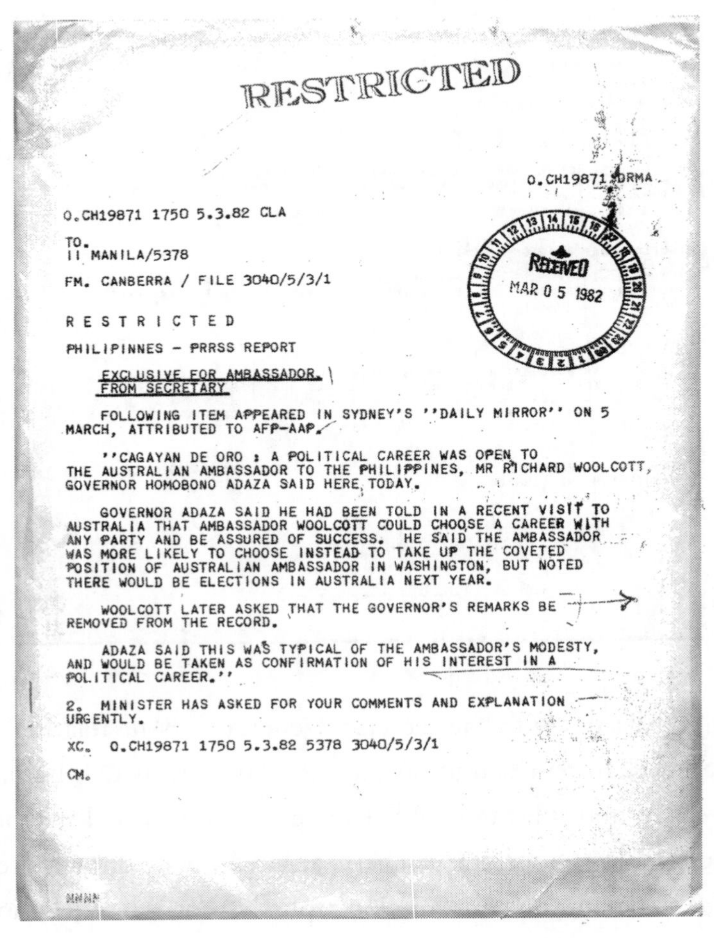

RESTRICTED

O.CH19871 DRMA.

O.CH19871 1750 5.3.82 CLA

RECEIVED MAR 05 1982

TO.
II MANILA/5378

FM. CANBERRA / FILE 3040/5/3/1

R E S T R I C T E D

PHILIPINNES - PRRSS REPORT

EXCLUSIVE FOR AMBASSADOR.
FROM SECRETARY

FOLLOWING ITEM APPEARED IN SYDNEY'S ''DAILY MIRROR'' ON 5 MARCH, ATTRIBUTED TO AFP-AAP.

''CAGAYAN DE ORO : A POLITICAL CAREER WAS OPEN TO THE AUSTRALIAN AMBASSADOR TO THE PHILIPPINES, MR RICHARD WOOLCOTT, GOVERNOR HOMOBONO ADAZA SAID HERE TODAY.

GOVERNOR ADAZA SAID HE HAD BEEN TOLD IN A RECENT VISIT TO AUSTRALIA THAT AMBASSADOR WOOLCOTT COULD CHOOSE A CAREER WITH ANY PARTY AND BE ASSURED OF SUCCESS. HE SAID THE AMBASSADOR WAS MORE LIKELY TO CHOOSE INSTEAD TO TAKE UP THE COVETED POSITION OF AUSTRALIAN AMBASSADOR IN WASHINGTON, BUT NOTED THERE WOULD BE ELECTIONS IN AUSTRALIA NEXT YEAR.

WOOLCOTT LATER ASKED THAT THE GOVERNOR'S REMARKS BE REMOVED FROM THE RECORD.

ADAZA SAID THIS WAS TYPICAL OF THE AMBASSADOR'S MODESTY, AND WOULD BE TAKEN AS CONFIRMATION OF HIS INTEREST IN A POLITICAL CAREER.''

2. MINISTER HAS ASKED FOR YOUR COMMENTS AND EXPLANATION URGENTLY.

XC. O.CH19871 1750 5.3.82 5378 3040/5/3/1

CM.

CHAPTER 16

Undiplomatic activities in the 21st century

This foreign policy stuff is a little frustrating.
— George W. Bush, 2002

As this century unfolds, I find I am living in a changed Australia. It is not the country I represented for four decades, usually with pride and always with dedication. Undiplomatic activities are not all amusing or lightly put aside. The enormity of the diplomatic errors of judgement in relation to Iraq would be a worthy subject for satire if the outcomes had not been so tragic and so current. It is, indeed, no laughing matter.

Australians can be proud of many of our achievements.

We are still a country of great potential and opportunity. Yet, in several areas we seem to have gone backwards over the last decade; our civil liberties certainly have been eroded in the name of the so-called war on terror. We seem to be sleepwalking into a surveillance society. It is in our own hands whether, in the years ahead, this drift toward a fearful and mean society can be arrested, and our potential as a decent, harmonious, tolerant, generous, and compassionate society can be fulfilled.

Throughout this book I have focused on the humorous aspects of diplomatic life. But laughter is hardly a proper response to some of the depressing developments in the world today: the unfolding horrors in Sudan; the proliferation of nuclear weapons; the increasing scourge of AIDS; and, of course, the Iraq misadventure which, as well as subjecting the country to terrible violence and an increasing number of civilian casualties, has exacerbated terrorism, religious intolerance, racism, and greed. Perhaps we are too close in time to them but I find it hard to find an amusing side to these situations.

President Bush, still a figure of fun to many, is more seriously a lame-duck president. As he wages an increasingly unpopular war respect for him internationally continues to decline. He finds himself confronted by a Congress controlled by Democrats determined not only to bring the troops home, but also to investigate all aspects of his administration's Iraq and Middle East policies. There is a strong possibility of a Democratic presidency in 2009. Sadly, for Australia, John Howard and Alexander Downer misjudged the capabilities of the Bush administration and eagerly tied their — and our — fortunes to a number of flawed American policies.

Now, like King Canute, Bush and his courtiers Dick Cheney, Tony Blair, John Howard, Alexander Downer, and more recently Brendan Nelson wait for the rising tide of political reality to submerge them. As a former Australian ambassador said last year, they find themselves 'up Shiite creek in a wire canoe without a paddle'.

As well as being complicit in the Iraq catastrophe, by

embracing the neo-conservative illusion of an era of United States global supremacy in which American ideas and ideals would prevail — and be imposed on rogue states, if necessary, by the pre-emptive use of force — the Australian government has permitted itself to be seen as remaining in the time-warp of the Anglosphere. The Howard government, following the US lead, has asserted its right to pre-emptive military action against terrorists in neighbouring countries, and reinforced perceptions that Australia welcomes the role of a 'deputy sheriff' in our region. It has also allowed itself to be seen as a bully in a number of smaller south-west Pacific countries.

I have always believed that self-delusion is a major threat to effective diplomacy. In an article in the *Australian Journal of International Affairs*, foreign minister Downer referred to the high regard in which Australia is held internationally. If we are indeed so respected in the international community, why have we been unable to secure election to the Security Council, the principal organ of the United Nations, since 1984?

After I retired from the public service, and especially after 1996, I became increasingly concerned about what has come to be called 'spin', and the employment by ministerial offices of an increasing number of 'spin-doctors' whose task it is to manage the news and to manipulate public opinion to suit their ministers' political interests. To a greater extent than I can ever remember, truth in government has been submerged in political spin and cover-up, especially — but not only — in matters related to Iraq.

For domestic political ends, the government has sought to anaesthetise the public and silence its foreign policy critics. Public diplomacy, long an important aspect of diplomatic activity, has been forced to concentrate on damage control. Sadly, the process has been debauched — mainly because of the government's determination to have its views prevail — by its intolerance of dissenting opinions, and by its support for the Bush administration's desire to mask the realities of the Iraq disaster.

We are enjoying the benefits of living in an economically

prosperous country, fuelled largely by China's economic boom and the international demand for our resources. But if our political culture is morally deficient and foreign policy follies like Iraq are not corrected this will inevitably undermine our standing.

Because I was the first public information officer appointed by the Department of External Affairs in 1964, I have always had a close personal interest in media liaison and briefing. While members of the press gallery often referred to me as the 'official leak', I was never accused of manipulating the truth. In fact, when I was appointed, the minister of the day, Sir Garfield Barwick, and the then head of the department, Sir Arthur Tange, insisted that the purpose of this new position was to promote a wider public understanding of Australian foreign policy. My role was to try to ensure that the government's position and the reasons behind it on any issue were known, but it was also made clear that this was not to involve the manipulation of public opinion on the basis of deception.

As leader of the Opposition, John Howard said in August 1995, 'Truth is absolute, truth is supreme, truth is never disposable in national political life.' This was a noble statement, but truth in government soon became a casualty of office with the children overboard affair, the invasion of Iraq, and its aftermath.

In recent times, ministers and their spin-doctors have

mislead journalists and then, to compound matters, appeared to believe the reports they themselves promoted. As John le Carré noted in his novel, *Absolute Friends*, 'Politicians lie to the press, see their lies printed and call them public opinion.'

The *Canberra Times* cartoonist Geoff Pryor summed up the situation well in a cartoon in October 2006 which showed Howard and Downer in a Land Rover bogged in the Iraqi desert. The back wheels are spinning and sand flying; an Arab standing nearby says to another, 'They've spun themselves in, let's see if they can spin themselves out.'

In trying to justify a failed policy, ministers and their spin-doctors often move the goal posts. They simply redefine their objectives rather than admit an error, or they change policy. For example, Prime Minister Howard said in March 2002, 'Our policy is the disarmament of Iraq, not the removal of Saddam Hussein.' He went further. A few days before the invasion in March 2003, he said that if Saddam got rid of his weapons of mass destruction (which he didn't have) he could remain in power. Later he changed his ground again saying that it would have been intolerable to allow such a brutal dictator as Saddam to remain in power.

In Washington, as casualties in Iraq mounted, spin doctors started to call body bags 'transfer tubes'. The word 'torture' needed to be avoided, so it was called 'extreme rendition' or 'active interrogation'. The many thousands of

Iraqi civilians killed or maimed, including women and children, starting with the US 'shock and awe' bombing campaign, are coldly dismissed as 'collateral damage'. Phrases like the 'defence of freedom and democracy' are used to mask such unsavoury events as the abuse of prisoners at Abu Ghraib. Unavoidable policy adjustments tend to be described as 'the construction of new realities'. President Bush's commitment of another 21,000 troops to Iraq in January 2007 in pursuit of his, by then, unachievable objectives was described not as a storm or a torrent, but only a 'surge'. This was intended to suggest to a critical public a temporary and limited increase — just enough to dispose of the evildoers disrupting Baghdad.

If public trust is to be restored in our democracy, disinformation, semantics, and deliberate ambiguity must never be used as a substitute for proper government briefing arrangements. Since retiring from the Department of Foreign Affairs and Trade, I have, with sadness, watched policy mistakes being repeated and earlier lessons forgotten or ignored.

At APEC in 2006, there was an obvious irony in seeing George Bush and John Howard meeting in Hanoi with their Vietnamese hosts. When Howard was a minister in the Fraser government, Hanoi had been seen as an enemy bent on destroying western influence — a role transferred to Iraq in 2002. In international diplomacy, as the French say,

Plus ça change, plus c'est la même chose.

plus ça change, plus c'est la même chose. The more things change, the more they remain the same.

Finally, the establishment of an Australian republic is not simply a constitutional issue. It has important symbolic as well as practical advantages for our international image, and for foreign and trade policies. I find it hard to comprehend that, seven years into the twenty-first century, John Howard and Alexander Downer are still self-declared monarchists, unlike Peter Costello, Malcolm Turnbull, and Kevin Rudd. Howard missed the great opportunity at the 1999 referendum to take the next great historic step in the unfolding story of Australia after Federation, to sever our anachronistic subservience to the British Crown, introduce an Australian republic, and become the prime minister who redefined Australia to ourselves and the world.

But despite these sad developments, I remain an optimist. Australian foreign policy — with its inevitable delinking from the Howard-Bush personal relationship — will inevitably be freer to adjust to a changing global situation. Policy will become more finely tuned, less ideological, and be shaped towards more appropriate balances in respect of the United States and other important countries in Asia. A more constructive approach to the United Nations will also strengthen our standing in multilateral diplomacy.

If so, we may all be able to laugh again at lesser follies.

sic transit gloria mundi

I first encountered the phrase *sic transit gloria mundi* when studying Latin at school. Gough Whitlam once informed me that the phrase is used during the coronation of a new pope. But, for me, it underlines the transitoriness of earthly successes so elegantly expressed in Shelley's poem 'Ozymandias'.

I have indeed been fortunate to have enjoyed such an eventful and interesting career in the Australian foreign service during which I was able to taste occasional success. It has been a fascinating journey for which I am enormously grateful to my family, who shared many of the experiences I have described, to friends and colleagues at home and abroad, and ultimately to the Australian people and taxpayers who made it possible.

Much as I appreciated the opportunities to learn more about the different cultures, systems, and societies of the one world in which we live, I always missed Australia, looked forward to home postings, and always wanted to end my days in this country of my birth which has given me so much.

Along with hard work and long hours, often in difficult circumstances or unfamiliar environments, there have also been many moments of joy, laughter and amusement, which I am pleased to share with readers.

I would particularly like to thank David Rowe for bringing some of those moments to life with his wonderful illustrations. Thanks also to my editor, Russ Radcliffe, whose efforts greatly improved the text, and to the staff at Scribe.